DEAR VALENTINA

BY MERLE AND VALENTINA MARTIN

EDITED BY TRACEY MATTESON TOENJES

FORTIS

AN ADDUCENT NON-FICTION IMPRINT
JACKSONVILLE, FLORIDA
WWW.ADDUCENT.CO

Dear Valentina

Merle and Valentina Martin

ISBN 978-1-937592-08-0

Published by Fortis (a Non-Fiction imprint from Adducent)

Jacksonville, Florida
www.Adducent.co (that's right, it's not a .com)
Published in the United States of America

TABLE OF CONTENTS

FOREWORD

I never met Merle Martin, but from January 2011 to January 2012, I got to know him very well. It didn't take long to realize how much he loved his wife and to what lengths he would go to in order to ensure her happiness. In reading his 300-plus letters during his service in World War II, I became witness to true love in its most genuine form, and it saddened me to think that people don't really talk like this anymore...and perhaps they don't love like this either.

Merle Martin's story is not incredibly dissimilar from those of many other WWII veterans. What makes this book incredibly unique and especially timely is what he conveys to his wife during a time of crisis—faith, hope, and love. It is somewhat disheartening to think that the kind of love expressed between husband and wife in this story is nowadays a sort of rarity. However, I am not completely discouraged by this because as I watched Val Martin wipe the tears from her eyes when I began reading the manuscript aloud to her, I realized that though Merle's words are over half a century old, the message they convey is everlasting. That gives me hope, hope that unfaltering love and faith can endure even the most challenging obstacles and retain its earnestness when to all others it would seem just a memory.

Tracey Matteson Toenjes

ACKNOWLEDGEMENTS

I am grateful first for the work of my typists, Cortney Caughlin, Breanna Helfrick, and Julie Schaefer whose crucial initial work launched this novel.

I also want to thank Dr. Jeffrey Copeland from the University of Northern Iowa for encouraging me to preserve and honor the memory of my husband and for setting an example himself of fine authorship. His support helped fuel this project from the first pages to the very last.

I am continuously grateful for our son, Jerald Martin, whose enthusiasm for his father's legacy kept the spirit of my work alive throughout this exciting and exhausting project and who faithfully safeguarded his father's letters during their Federal Express trip to the U.S. Library of Congress where he and others can visit them and continue to observe the story they honor.

Lastly, I am thankful for my brilliant editor, Tracey Matteson Toenjes, for her time, knowledge, patience, and effort in turning my dream into a reality. Her obsessive commitment to Merle's story and mine resulted in what you read now.

LOVE IS THE CLIMAX OF MY HAPPINESS
AND THE PINNACLE OF MY PAIN.

LOVE IS THE FIRE IN MY HEART WITH AN
ETERNAL FLAME.

-UNKNOWN

PROLOGUE

That day, December 15, 1944—our third anniversary—was a great gift for a married couple, but it was also a day we would remember as our own "day of infamy." When I arrived at Camp Joseph T. Robinson near Little Rock, Arkansas, I had only a few moments to kiss my nearly new husband goodbye. Neither of us knew whether he would ever return to the United States. In order to get to him, I had to pass under a row of soldiers on both sides of the path leading to him, under crossed guns and bayonets near the P.X.

Saying goodbye to Merle when I might never see him again was so very sad and heart breaking for both of us. It brought an unavoidable flood of tears. We both cried and hung onto each other. Everyone—the other couples there too—was crying and clinging together for a few last moments. Merle and I both attempted to be strong for each other, but the tears fell anyway; it was particularly poignant because it this day was our third anniversary. We were frightened, and the armed guards did nothing to make us feel safer or happier. The two of us leaned on each other until I was ordered to leave.

I suppose that I was still crying on the way back to Little Rock. I must have pulled myself together because, still in a state of shock, I managed to buy a train ticket back to Iowa at the station and load my steamer trunk—from which I had been living while Merle was stationed at previous military bases—into a taxi. Like Merle, I was on my way into a lonely, dark, and foreboding future.

Merle was drafted on September 25, 1942, years before our tearful goodbye. His first assignment was basic training at Fort Sill in Lawton, Oklahoma. As he put on his first uniform at

MERLE AND VALENTINA MARTIN

Camp Dodge, Iowa (now in Johnston), there was a sign on top of the mirror which read, "You are now looking at the finest soldier in the world." He asked, "How could that be when every piece of clothing is either big or *too* big?" After his basic training, he became a soldier on the 45th Artillery Division of the U.S. Army which had been the original Oklahoma National Guard. He lived at the base while I lived in a room in Lawton and worked at a Kresge's "five-and-dime," a then once-well-known national chain of stores. Bob and Velma, our old friends from Camp Pickett, were nearby, and we met new friends as well.

In January, 1943, the 45th Division was alerted to go into the European Theater of War. Merle left on a darkened troop train from Fort Sill, heading toward the eastern United States. We owned a four-door 1940 Chevy, and I was to follow the troop train with it. I would stop at major cities, beginning with the Chattanooga, Tennessee Western Union office to find out what the next Western Union office would be as my destination, which Merle indicated in each telegram he sent me. The next telegram would direct me to the next station and so-on until both of us reached Camp Pickett in Blackstone, Virginia. While there, Merle would bivouac with the 45th Division artillery for overseas duty.

I then found a job as a hostess and a cashier at a Greek-owned restaurant in Blackstone. We made more Army friends like Ed Garabidian, a sergeant at the hospital who loved to have fun. We danced to "Good Old Cabbage Greens" at the Waynotta Inn—named after Nottaway County where it was located. The owners were Woodrow and Hallie Martin. For a while, Merle guarded the bus station as a military police officer while we were stationed at Camp Pickett with the 45th division. After a few months at Camp Pickett, the station hospital needed the help of a mechanic, so Merle became a member of the Camp Pickett Hospital maintenance staff. We thought that this was going to be a permanent assignment for the duration of the war.

After we got used to life in Virginia, we received a 30-day furlough in June 1944. We went home, and on our fourth day in Iowa, the church bells peeled—it was D-Day in Normandy, European Theater of War. At the time, we were at my parents' farm with our dog, Toy. After the furlough, we were transferred to Camp Ellis in Macomb, Illinois. At Camp Ellis, Merle and most of the other men employed in the hospital at Camp Pickett joined the 74th Field Hospital which was under the leadership of Colonel Damron. Merle then started plumbing school; they apparently needed toilets wherever he was going, though we knew not where. His aptitude for mechanics of any kind came from his tinkering in a neighbor's garage while he was in high school. It later proved to be an invaluable skill.

Living in the hedonistic wartime atmosphere of "eat, drink, and be merry, for tomorrow we may die," Velma, Bob, Merle, and I decided to have a party in the mammoth apartment that Bob and Velma had rented. We invited all the men of the 74th Field Hospital, who had already been alerted on December 1st that they were about to be sent overseas for the Japanese Theater of War. We had nearly the entire outfit there, eating good food and drinking good wine. We had a ball at that party, visiting and meeting people from all over the entire nation. It all had to end of course, and at midnight, one of the soldiers—Ralph Byers—picked up our guests in an Army 6x6 truck to take them back to camp.

The 74th Field Hospital was transported by darkened troop trains to Fort Lewis, Washington (about 45 miles south of Seattle). At that time, Merle and I still didn't know where he was going. It was a cruel irony for Merle that his troop train came through our home town of Waterloo, Iowa only a few days after I had arrived there. A 17-year-old soldier from Williamsport, Indiana, later told me that Merle's friends had asked this boy to watch Merle so that he wouldn't jump off the slow-moving train and go AWOL to see me. He said that Merle's eyes were filled with long and big tears, but after leaving Waterloo, he had resigned himself to continue to their destination.

On Christmas Day, 1944, Merle called me and told me that he was leaving to go overseas, and he ended up in Camp Koko Head, Oahu in the Hawaiian Islands. Later, I discovered that he had left the United States shortly after Christmas on the *U.S.S. President Johnson*, converted into a troop ship. The 74th Field

Hospital was to see jungle training and of course, another bivouac.

Some time before March 17, 1945, Merle sailed from Hawaii on the *U.S.S. Okanogan* for many days in a convoy, stalling for time to invade Okinawa with at least 1,250 other ships of all kinds waiting offshore. The *Okanogan* stopped at Ulithi in the Caroline Islands. Some of the soldiers got off the ship to visit. Merle stayed on board and wrote to me about the beautiful moon and calm sea—both of us looking at the same moon. The weather now was tropical, according to his letters. The *U.S.S. Okanogan* stopped at Eniwetok, but the tide was not right to get off there. These letters, of course, have no dates on them since their commanding officer told the men that they could not date their letters.

The motor pool of 16 men which Merle would later join was on the *U.S.S. Valencia*. Their voyage was somewhat different. They too were stalling to coordinate their arrival with that of the U.S. Navy fleet armada for "Love Day," the day they landed for Operation: Iceberg, the invasion of Okinawa on April 1, 1945, Easter Sunday and April Fools' Day. Merle and the rest of the rest of the 74th Field Hospital arrived 17 days later.

The *Okanogan* stalled for nearly a month, although the destroyers of the Navy had been bombing and shelling Okinawa to soften the beach-head prior to the arrival of the many supply ships and personnel headed there. On the 17th of April, they landed on Yellow Beach to dig their foxholes and set up the tents and equipment of the 74th Field Hospital. Setting up a hospital with no electricity was a terrific challenge for the men attached to the unit. The entire island was 65 miles long and only four miles wide at its narrowest point. Merle was busy setting up electrical systems with gasoline generators, often digging a foxhole near what he hoped would be his tent. He was the technician responsible for the lights, along with a crew of other soldiers in his squad. The Field Hospital was only 1,200 yards behind the field of battle so that it could swiftly provide care for wounded soldiers. They were always brought to the field hospitals first. According to Bob Peterson of Westminster, Maryland, the Staff

Sergeant in the 74th surgery unit, 97% of those treated in the field hospitals survived.

After the injured were able to be moved, they were sent by air from Yontan or Kadena airfields to Saipan, Guam, or to the *U.S.S. City of Hope*, a Red Cross hospital ship in the bay. If they recovered quickly, they were returned to battle. If they were too severely wounded, they were sent back to the United States, a trip Merle so badly wanted so he could come home.

Merle was not happy with the war but felt that it was his duty to his family and country to leave home and fight. I am his wife, the author of his memory, and the collector of his letters which tell his story, the pain of war, and our love for each other.

Merle Martin

DECEMBER 1944

It's easy to tell how naive we both were even at that time. Here was my husband going into the unknown parts of the world, and it seemed like the end of my life. I was as much in love with him as he was with me. We had been so involved with each other up until this point.

Of course, neither of us knew where Merle was going. We knew only that he was headed for the Pacific Theater of Operations. He was eventually sent to Okinawa. My personal research discovered that while I was on my way to Iowa and Merle on his way to the western United States, a typhoon was raging in the Pacific.[1] This, the first of two typhoons to batter the Third Fleet, did significant damage to the American forces in spite of the immense power of the United States Navy at that time.

Admiral William Halsey's Third Fleet had gone from victory to victory over the Japanese Navy—a magnificent achievement, but despite the first-rate equipment and the tremendous skill of his Navy personnel, a simple misreading of a barometer led to the dispatching of Task Force 38, Halsey's strongest assault force, commanded by Vice-Admiral John Sidney McCain[2]—directly into the heart of a horribly destructive storm that struck in the Philippine Sea on December 18, 1944, a few days after Merle and I left Little Rock.

---

1   The first of two typhoons that damaged the U.S. Navy's Third Fleet in the Pacific struck on December 17-18, 1944. The second came on June 2-3, 1945, east of Okinawa.
2   Vice-Admiral McCain was the father of another Four-Star Admiral, John S. McCain, Jr., and the grandfather of Senator John McCain, the Republican nominee for President of the United States in the November 2008 election.

DEAR VALENTINA

Halsey ordered Task Force 38, a force of seven enormous aircraft-carriers, six light carriers, eight battleships and some 70 cruisers and destroyers—along with their attendant landing ships and support crafts—to rendezvous with another element of the fleet about 300 miles east of Luzon in the Philippine Sea. His motive was to refuel at sea because of the distance from any refueling port. He wanted to avoid any threat to the fleet by Japanese aircraft which he considered the greatest danger to the invasion. The winds began to rise on December 17, and all operations such as refueling, repairs, the transfer of personnel, etc., immediately became much more difficult and dangerous.

Halsey suggested that the next day, December 18, might be safer for those operations because refueling at sea is extremely hazardous even in the calmest waters. Over a period of falling barometer readings, the typhoon's winds grew fiercer. Within a short time, three destroyers had been sunk, and numerous other ships badly damaged, with the loss of approximately 800 men. At least 146 aircrafts on the carrier were destroyed.

The storm, of course, had nothing to do with the "Divine Wind"—*kamikaze* in Japanese—the legendary typhoon in the 13th century which destroyed the Mongol fleets on their way to invade Japan. Later during the war, the suicide pilots and their aircraft took the name of the kamikaze when they set out on suicide missions which destroyed many ships and killed hundreds of United States servicemen.

This tragedy was a great blow to the U.S. Navy and the forces under Halsey's command on their mission to invade Okinawa, which is situated in an area typically stricken by typhoons between April and December each year. The American forces were apparently unaware of this phenomenon.

All this took place when Merle was on his way to Fort Lewis, Washington, a destination of which he and his fellow soldiers were completely unaware. December of 1944 was a sad month for the two newlyweds—married for only three years. Five days after he left, Merle wrote me my first letter which had a six-cent air-mail stamp, censored despite the fact that he was still riding a blacked-out troop train.

MERLE AND VALENTINA MARTIN

Dec. 20, 1944
Sweetie Pie:

We are in the West and I'm O.K. only lonesome for you. I haven't taken a bath yet and I'm pretty dirty, but that doesn't hurt me any. I'm looking around for something for you as a little present but haven't found anything yet. Maybe I can get you a [censored]. I was pretty lucky since I last saw you, I picked up about $75. I will send you some money home as soon as possible to even up my account as we talked about.

Hope you arrived safely and had a nice trip.

I'm not feeling very good lately as my back hurts me but I guess I'll live. Did Dad receive the package I sent him? Tell him to use any thing of mine he wants to. Be sure to get the folks something for Xmas and tell them instead of getting me anything give you money and we can spend that together. As far as your concerned don't deprive yourself of anything you need, just be a good little girl and wait for daddy.

I don't have time to write the folks today but will write them soon. When you receive this letter, call the folks and let them know I'm O.K. I will write you again tonite and every day so let me hear from you just as often. Go to the drug store and see if you can get me some 620 Verichrome films as one of the boys have a Kodak and we can take some pictures to send home. By the way I want you to have your picture taken and put in one of those little folders so I can carry you in my pocket all the time. Ha. Well, Ma! This is all for now but will write you a political letter tonite. Ha! Be good and God Bless you, Honey!

Poppa loves every ounce of you to the bottom of his heart.
Bye Mommy!
With all my love
Merle

"Coconut" was the word censored, probably alluding to Hawaii. Censorship was new to me. Merle soon reached Fort Lewis after our emotional farewell. Undoubtedly, he and others received an early pay-day because they would soon be leaving the United States. They shot craps and played poker on the way.

DEAR VALENTINA

Dear Mommy:

I wrote you this afternoon, but I'll write again to tell you anything I left out. I want to be sure you hear from me every day, and you better write me every nite before you go to bed or I'll paddle your canoe for you. Ha! When I hear from you and find out you are well and as happy as the war will permit you to be, it makes my mind at ease. I wrote the folks tonite and spoke to them about you keeping the radio.

By the way when you write only write on one side of the paper. You can write anything you want to, so be sure and keep me up on all the news. The censors won't allow me to say everything I want to. When you write, don't miss one thing and tell me everything that happens back home.

Well, this is all for tonite, Honey, but will write two more tomorrow. Keep your chin up, your nose clean, be a sweet mommy, and keep the letters coming. Here's a good-nite kiss and I'll see you in my dreams. God Bless You my Darling - Wife. With Every Ounce of My Love
Merle

That letter was one of my first "God bless you" letters, though Merle's family never belonged to a church. When he and I married, he began attending my Catholic church. I knew he was interested and seemed to enjoy the Latin masses. Now the idea of God began soaking into his soul. Most likely, his love for me was making it possible. He needed the tranquility in his life during our separation by war and now began to feel a risk by having to leave the country. He liked the closeness of family and the cohesion of relatives that were open and have meaningful discussions. His father, one of seven boys of a widowed mother, was respectful of everyone, particularly his wife, by building a church of love and felt that the biggest compliment to a husband was to love his children's mother. I was young and thought of my love for my good looking soldier. I became increasingly aware of how much I loved him and how much he loved me.

Merle was realizing what a serious situation he was in, now that the war had suddenly become more real to him. I was not catching on yet. He sensed that we might indeed need divine help to survive it intact. What he wanted and needed most, however, was a letter from me, and at least one every day if possible. At that time, it was impossible for me to write him, because he was in limbo. He had no address—everything that could present even the remotest possibility of giving information to the enemy was kept secret.

I was surprised just before Christmas when I received $500 from Merle by way of a Western Union telegram. On the next day, another $500 check was sent to me by telegram from Merle. On the third day, Western Union delivered yet another telegram from Merle. This time, he asked me to send *him* $500, because his luck had run out, and now he was really missing the money that he had so generously sent me.

Oh! I sent you a little present of Sixty dollars by wire today, of course, you'll receive it long before this letter, I could have sent more, but I thought I'd keep back a little for some necessary things and I also want to open up an account called "The Soldiers Account." You just give what ever you want to your commanding officer and have a bank book the same as any bank book. The money draws 4% interest and you can draw it out when it is needed. I want to save all I can so when I get back you and I can walk down the street and see all those nice dresses in the windows, we can buy them for Mommy dear. How about it?

He also asked me for a "pin-up" photo of me that I had taken for him after my return to Iowa. "Pin-up" girls—photos of wives, sweethearts, and movie-stars, made popular by Hollywood star, Betty Grable—were a favorite amongst the troops, and the term "Pin-up" is one that recalls memories of WWII for most of those who lived through it in the United States and abroad.

DEAR VALENTINA

Val's pin-up picture from National Studio in Waterloo, Iowa.

Dec. 21, 1944
Sweetheart!

Just finished a game of checkers with the Major so will drop you a line before going to bed.

This "Major" who Merle mentions would end up being his roommate at their final destination. Nate Johnson would prove to be a dedicated friend and good company to Merle throughout his experiences overseas.

I don't know why I can't get enough sleep. I'm tired all the time. Of course it's nothing unusual for me to be lazy, isn't it, Ma! By the way how do you like my stationery? I bought it

5

special for you, so you see I'm thinking of you all the time. I kinda looked for a letter from you today and went along with Johnson to the post-office but came back disappointed. That better not happen too much.

I expect to arrange to send some money to you tomorrow by wire as I have too much on me and I have to keep too close watch on my pocket-book. I suppose there is plenty of snow and ice back home and maybe you think I wouldn't like to be back there throwing snow-balls at you. But this war won't last forever and we'll sure make up for lost time when I get back there. I'm going to save every cent I can get hold of so I can get you any thing you want when I get back.

You can tell your folks hello for me because I'm going to address all my mail to you and you can tell every-one else the news. Of course you can tell Betty, Valeria and the rest of the family to write me because mail is all that will keep my moral up, and especially that from my truthful and Sweet little Wife who sure has been a faithful pal to me for three years and I know she'll continue for thirty or forty more even though I'm not there.

Oh! yes has Valeria heard from Dave yet?

Betty and Valeria, to whom he refers often in his letters, were my two younger sisters. He wanted me to urge them to write him letters too. These letters from all of us back home were essential to maintaining his morale; he was isolated from all that was familiar and on his way to a place of mortal danger. Such a request was easy to understand. He was especially anxious to hear from my sister Valeria to get information about her husband—his good friend and brother-in-law, Dave—to whom he often referred to as "Pookey" in his letters. Merle wanted to write him as soon as possible because Merle was sensing that Dave would soon be sent overseas as well. Dave was serving with a U.S. Marine division heading to the South Pacific.[3]

---

3 Dave left our hometown on November 5, 1944 to serve with the U.S. Marines in the 3rd Division. He was killed on March 3, 1945.

DEAR VALENTINA

On December 22, 1944, the 74th Field Hospital held a Christmas party for its soldiers in their barracks at Fort Lewis. Gifts such as hair oil, toothbrushes, and other toiletries—possibly supplied by the Red Cross—also included decks of cards that without question came in handy after the Battle of Okinawa would end. Merle missed me at the party, but he said that we'd be together again by the next Christmas 1945, despite having no clear idea of where he was being sent. He did not make the next Christmas either. He also wanted his brother-in-law Dave's address. I did not hear from Merle again until I got an urgent phone call from him on Christmas Day. He had spent Christmas Eve Day and most of Christmas Day trying to reach me by phone and finally managed to get a call through to me at his parents' home, very late in the day. Of course, we could hardly talk because we were both crying. My idea about getting that call is that he must have known that he was going to embark after Christmas. My own "Merry Christmas" telegram to him reached him at Fort Lewis, Washington.

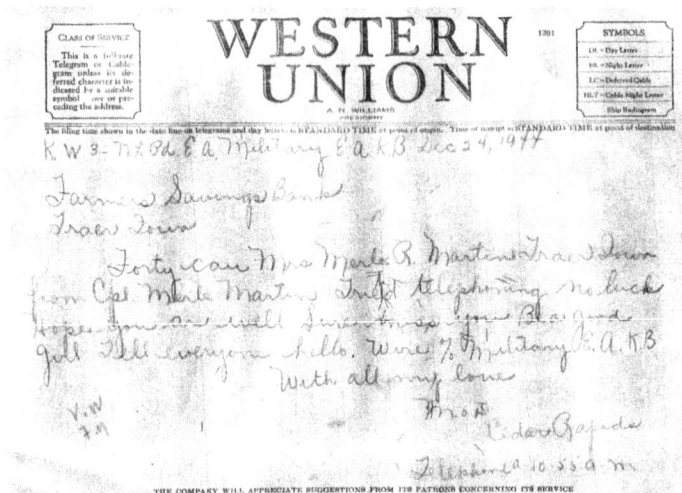

Western Union Christmas Telegram to Val from Merle on December 24, 1944

I just got back to the barracks from a little gathering of all the members of our unit, in other words kind of a little Xmas gathering. We all received gifts. I got some hair oil, after shave lotion, a deck of cards, envelopes and such things as that. It surely helped a lot. Only one thing was wrong and that was I didn't have my mommy there in person, but believe me, she was there in my heart and a 100% too. I know we will be able to celebrate next Xmas together as the world can't keep us apart only so long, we won't allow it, will we, Honey?

Dec. 24, 1944
6:30 PM
To my Darling Wife: (on Xmas Eve!)
      "Merry Xmas, Honey!"
      Mommy I've been sitting here at the telephone office since nine o'clock this morning trying to get a call thru to you. I still have hopes as the office doesn't close until 10:30, but if I don't get to talk to you tonite, I'll call again tomorrow. I also intend to send you some more money by wire tomorrow. Gee! what I wouldn't give to get a hold of you and hug and kiss the devil out of you. I know it's impossible, but anyway I can dream, can't I?

      Last nite passes were available until midnite so Gus, Johnson and myself went into town. We bought the best meal we could, took in a show and shopped for something to send home, but everything was pretty well picked over, so I'll just send some more money to mamma. We received a partial payment yesterday so you know there were crap games going on in every corner. I was charge of quarters, but I still managed to get in a few good rolls.

      Well, I just received bad news they got my call through but no one answered. I was calling you at Mary Wilson. Now I am down-hearted. I told her to try again in the morning but tomorrow being Xmas I don't have much hopes. I just went up to send you a telegram and happen to ask if there was any word for me and your answer to my first telegram was there. You can't imagine how much better I feel hearing from you. It seems to give me a relieved feeling.

      Honey I know it's going to be hard on you, but I know you will do as I ask, and all I ask is to spend all your spare time *writing to me. I've sent you enough money so that you can write me six air mail letters for one year and I sure don't intend to be away from you that long so why don't you double up and write twelve a day. By the way I still haven't received a letter from you. The other thing I ask is not to run around <u>at all</u> so I don't have to worry. I don't mean not to go to a show but don't go any other place like a dance or something like that. You'll promise me that, won't you, Honey? You know I won't be tearing around any or even have a place to sleep like you. Visit my folks a lot because I know it will make them feel good to have you around. You know they are both very sensitive about something like that. You also should know by now that there is nothing they wouldn't do for you.*

Gus and Johnson are still waiting to get a call through to their wives but I'm afraid they won't have any luck either. Walle hasn't tried to call his wife, or Weaver either, I guess they are too stingy. You know Walle sure acts funny towards us three lately. We can't figure out what's wrong with him.

I offered to give the telephone girl $20 tonite if she'd get you on the line so I could talk to you on Xmas eve and she tried too, but no dice.

Well I guess I've wrote a book to you and still haven't said anything but I surely enjoy pouring my heart out to you every day. I'm going to go take a shower and shave so I can be up to the telephone office early tomorrow and sweat out another call to you. At least I can spend Xmas trying to talk with you whether I can or not.

Again Merry Xmas "Darling Wife" and here's a big hug and a million kisses for you Honey! Be a good girl and write me a couple books each and every day. "God Bless You, Mommy".
With Every Ounce of my Love
Merle
P.S. I'll write you a special letter on Xmas Day.

Dec. 25, 1944
Merry Xmas Darling:

Merle and Valentina Martin

Here I am still sweating out a telephone call to you. I spent all day yesterday and I've been here all day today. I missed my breakfast and supper also. I did take time to go eat turkey dinner at the mess hall. They got thru to Traer this A.M. about 11:30 (our time) but found out you were in Waterloo so I changed the call to there. I don't know if I'll get thru tonite but if I don't, they will have to throw me out of this place at closing time.

I'm glad to hear you were spending Xmas at the folks and I know it will make a happier Xmas for them. I hope you had a nice time only if I could have been in that vacant chair. Gee Mommy hurry up and stop this war so I can come home to you.

Gus and Johnson finally got to talk to their wives about midnite last nite. They said it surely made them feel happy.

We had a swell turkey dinner today at the mess hall and all the trimmings that go with it.

I did not hear from Merle again until I got an urgent phone call from him on Christmas Day. He had spent Christmas Eve Day and most of Christmas Day trying to reach me by phone and finally managed to get a call through to me at his parents' home very late in the day. Of course, we could hardly talk because we were both crying.

Well, Honey! I got to talk to you last nite and that was worth a million. I knew it would be a sad conversation but at least I could talk to you. I couldn't finish this letter last nite because I was too upset.

Merle's Christmas letter expresses his continued attempts to find closeness to God. His customary "God bless you" in his closings became very familiar to me for many months. His letters were extremely passionate, for he undoubtedly knew that he would soon be leaving the United States for a very dangerous destination that remained a mystery to us both for many weeks to come.

Merle in uniform, either big or too big.

January 1945

In January, I received the first letter after Merle's and my conversation on Christmas Day from Fort Lewis, Washington. He was now able to tell me about going through our hometown a few days after I arrived and wanted so badly to see me from the darkened troop train. Above all, he finally told me that he was headed for Fort Lewis for embarkation to the South Pacific.

January 7, 1945
To My Darling Wife:

Hello Mommy! I hope this letter finds you well and happy and I know you'll be anxious to get it as this is the first opportunity I've had to write since I left the U. S. When ever the man says write I surely do my share. I also didn't have much luck in hearing from you until yesterday. Up until then I had received only one letter from you, and maybe you think I didn't memorize that. Yesterday I rung the bell and received thirteen letters from you. Boy you can't imagine how it makes me feel to hear from you. "Darling," I read all of them twice so I wouldn't miss anything. Today I received two V-mail from you, one from Betty and two from Mother. A total of 18 letters. I could cry I was so happy. I just as well be honest and tell you I did cry when I read them.

Mommy I am now permitted to tell you a few things so here goes. I went thru our home town shortly after you arrived. Maybe you think I didn't grit my teeth. I looked for you as I passed thru but of course I didn't see you. We left from Seattle, W. I also am some where in the Pacific. Don't worry because I'm perfectly safe. I am also permitted to tell you that I have seen plenty of coconuts. Maybe later I can tell you exactly where I'm at.

Merle bought cigars for my dad, Jerry, but was not permitted to mail them. In the letter he told me he wanted me to stay with his folks but did not want me to work at the John Deere Tractor Company nor Rath Packing Company. John Deere was making parts for airplanes and Jeeps. Rath was shipping meat to the armed forces at various APO (American Post Office) numbers to all the war theaters of operation to feed our armed forces.

The trip Merle left on the *U.S.S. President Johnson* heading west on the Pacific Ocean was rough. He was more seasick than lovesick on that trip. Many soldiers of the 74th who were sailing on the *President Johnson* were so seasick. Leaving solid ground was a sad experience since they were leaving the United States behind, although weather was fine, so they were sadly able to see the Seattle skyline disappear.

The latrines were very busy. It was raining, and the decks were slippery, and of course, the 74th land lubbers got very seasick. No lights were allowed on the account of security. Merle wrote that he was terribly seasick and that the food was bad and the rough sea made it worse.

By New Year's Day, the troops were feeling better. They had turkey, dressing, and all the trimmings, but many were still not very hungry while on board the *President Johnson.*

The ship docked the night of January 6, 1945. The troops were put on a truck for Camp Koko Head Hawaii Medical Concentration Camp. That is where the soldiers' mattress covers were issued but with no mattresses. Merle then figured out the real purpose of issuing mattress covers. They were to be used as body bags in case anyone would be killed. Merle threw his overboard before he left the *U.S.S. President Johnson.* He was determined to come back without needing a body bag to get him home. While Merle was aboard the ship, I had not been able to have any contact with him.

A letter finally arrived after January 7th. Until then, after our Christmas conversation, there was no mail. During this time,

I felt so alone and isolated to be without my kind and loving husband. I wrote a lot of letters and listened to the radio to find out where he was to ultimately set up the field hospital. I had my parents, my sisters, and my in-laws for support. For my own sake, I felt safe. My sister was with her husband in the Naval Base in Oceanside, California. She also would be returning to our parents' home.

Writing long letters to Merle daily was my most important activity. I missed him desperately. Just like he was waiting to hear from me, I waited anxiously for mail from him every day.

The soldiers were permitted to write the day after they landed on Koko Head, and they were very happy to be on land again. In Hawaii, there was a lot to see and do. They could go swimming on Minnesota Beach a few yards from camp. Shortly after they arrived at Camp Koko Head, the first thing they had to do was start unpacking. After eating in another mess hall, their own mess hall was opened. Now they received their new APO Number: 17928. Quarantine was lifted, and 15% of the men received passes. The 74th lost their nurses who were sent to Saipan to help with mid-Pacific casualties.

The rest of the men worked on getting into good physical condition in preparation for combat. Most of the time was spent in leisure as well as enjoying good food. Merle went shopping for me. He wanted to buy me more than he could afford. They also partied with cokes and beer, and one of the soldiers poured a can of ice water on one of his own boys.

DEAR VALENTINA

Camp Koko Head, Hawaii. Left-right: Gusler, Merle, Johnson, Lt. Musick

On first impression, most of the soldiers liked what they saw and were pleased to be there. Open air theater movies became available to them. Merle's first night he did not go to a movie but wrote me a love letter like so many that would follow to make sure I received one for each day he was gone although some were lost on sunken ships, but not many even though the war was on. However, because he was on a secret mission, he was not receiving any mail, primarily because he was in transit. I was lonely and lovesick as well, but I kept writing. Many letters were ten to twelve days late because of the secretive mission and the various other reasons the Army delayed them.

He mentions Ireta, his brother's sister-in-law in New York of whom Merle was not very fond. She had been through several marriages and many times needed Merle's sister-in-law to help her get over them.

Merle's uncle, Ben, died shortly after Merle reached Hawaii. Of course, I went to the funeral. His cousin, Mildred who had been his childhood playmate wrote him a letter when I gave her his address. She and I met for the first time after the funeral. I liked her a lot because she taught me so much about my husband that I didn't already know.

During January 1945, I was looking for a job while Merle was sending letters from Hawaii. On January 8th, he was writing me a letter from his barracks. Up until then, he had not been able to write for security reasons after the horrible weather he had experienced the few days after he left Puget Sound. At that time, none of us—Merle, the field hospital, or myself—knew where he was headed yet.

These were anxious days for me of not knowing and not hearing from him, so I just kept writing.

On January 13th, he was permitted to tell me about the voyage to Oahu, Hawaii from Fort Lewis, Washington. How sick he was and memories of our life together kept coming back particularly that day we left the PX (Post Exchange) in Little Rock, Arkansas on our third anniversary.

He wanted the address for his brother-in-law, Dave at Marine Headquarters so he could make contact with him because both of them could possibly be going to the same place in the Pacific Theater of Operations. To me, Merle was acting like fear was constantly moving through him.

Jan. 13, 1945
To My Darling Wife:

Hello Honey! Just came home from a free show so will write to you before going to bed. We have open air shows here in camp. They are pretty good considering that they are free. Bob Hope was on tonite.

Honey I am now permitted to tell you where I am. We are on the island of Oahu in Hawaii (I don't mean Wampoo either, Ha!). We were allowed to write where we are today. It isn't so bad here but not like people say it is. Honolulu is just a few miles away. We are allowed one pass a week from 11 A.M. to 10 P.M. There is nothing in town only hot dog stands and expensive souvenirs. I haven't been in as yet but Johnson and I intend to go one day next week. All we want to go for is to get something to send home. We have ridden thru town and can plainly see there is nothing for us there. I have a luncheon cloth and six napkins which come in sets to get for you, also I found a pillow top with Hawaii and palm trees drawn on them. They are really nice just so they aren't all gone when we get there. I also understand there are a few Parker pen and pencil sets in town so if I find one I'll get it for you. Outside of that one has no business in town only to throw away money and get into trouble. A person is better off in camp anyway because he gets his three meals a day, a PX is close by and a free movie every nite. A person can get along OK even though it isn't like home and a married man has no business looking for anything more. Isn't that true Darling? At least that's the way I feel about it.

I surely wish I could get in contact with Dave but don't know if I will be able to or not. It is not as easy as it sounds. Now that I'm able to say where I'm at, I'm going to write to him tomorrow and then when I go to town next week I'm going to the Red Cross and see if they can help me locate him. If he's on a different Island than I am I'll probably not be able to find him. Tell Valeria not to feel hurt if I don't because it won't be because I didn't try. I'd surely get a kick out of talking over old times with him myself. You know that is about the only enjoyment we have over here is to talk about how we used to do.

MERLE AND VALENTINA MARTIN

Jan. 14, 1945
Darling Wife:

Hello Mommy! How are you on this bright and sun shinny Sunday? I hope well and sweet as you used to be. Gusler just got the bright idea to write you a letter. So he wrote it and I censored it as you will see my initials on the bottom. I don't know if you will be able to read his writing or not but I guess if you can figure mine out you won't have any trouble with his.

Oh yes! I sent you a cablegram today. We can pick out any three messages of 190 so I tryed to pick out the three of the sweetest to send to you.

We sat around the tent and had a big discussion how true or untrue our wives could and would be while we were apart. There were about six of us and it ended up in a pretty good argument before we were finished. When I got the floor I told them if they didn't have a wife they knew would be true to them while they were away fighting for their country they had no use being married and they didn't even have a wife they just had a temporary bed partner. It made a couple of them mad but that is what I meant. I'm sure Darling you won't make me out a Liar in the slightest way, will you?

When Merle left the United States, he and his friend Gusler were having pains in their arms and legs. Today you would expect that from older men, not twenty-three- and twenty-nine-year-old boys. All of us hoped their ailments would get them sent to a hospital or home. Still fearful, Gusler even wrote me a letter from Hawaii under Merle's watchful eye.

14 January 1944
Dear Valle,

This husband of yours isn't worth a dam. I wanted to start the letter, but the 'son of a gun' insulted me and wouldn't even let me use his pen and paper.

Everything is pretty nice here on the island. If we could only get away from some of the associates we brought from the States with us. When we go "down under" which is a famous expression here, anything could hapen. That is what we are living for now.

Tonight is Sunday night, but things are different here. There are no wine cellars to break into. Spirits are very hard to get. I think I will be a prohibitionist after this war.

Your husband is reading this over my shoulder and I don't like it one bit. I think it is better then you won't have to send it back to him for approval. Nothing like having a husband to censor your mail.

I got a letter from Robbie Wallauer. She seemed to be fairly happy. I hope she does fair in the WACS again. Little Rock isn't my idea of an ideal place to live. Guess I am old fashioned. If you can figure this out you are a wizzard. Wish I could have known you better but your husband is very selfish and I can't say as I blame him.

I should become a daddy most any day now and the letter I got from my wife today said that she would be sure that Mrs. Martin got an announcement. So you see that I am between a lather and a sweat now wondering whether it will be a boy or girl. My wife still says it will be a boy. More power to the Guslers. By the time I get out of this war, I will probably be to old to try again. But nothing can stop one from dreaming or thinking. "Isn't nature wonderful"!

Martin says he wants you to be busy for a week so if you can transcribe this I think you will be a nervous wreck by Sunday.

I expect an answer and my address is the same as Merle's.

So long

Gus

(Passed by censor MRM. Merle R. Martin)

"Robbie" in Gusler's letter was our friend Velma. She was married to "Wally" or Bob. Later, Velma would join the Women's Army Corps or "WACs," a dirty word to many people in those days.

Merle and Valentina Martin

Hawaii was beautiful when they drove around the island. The flowers of all kinds grew promiscuously because of the warm and damp climate. Merle wrote that he would like his mother and me to see them. He and Gusler drove to another camp since Gusler was a sergeant in charge of supplies and spent time sightseeing on Oahu. He saw a hotel on the beach and decided he wanted to stay with me there some day. After our 40th wedding anniversary, we did just that.

Bob (Wally) posing for a battle shot.

DEAR VALENTINA

In Hawaii there was plenty of down time for the 74th, so many soldiers worked on hobbies. Merle built himself a writing table with a drawer in which to keep his writing supplies. He was quite capable and adept at carpentry, and his skills came in handy when he and the boys needed things done.

Our old friends from Camp Pickett were writing to both Merle and me. One was a gentleman who used to eat in the Greek-owned restaurant where I worked. Olin Wade was a gentleman who worked at Camp Pickett for the railroad. Another man by the name of Ray Jarman was another whose letters meant so much to Merle as they would to all servicemen when they were away from home. Many wrote me for Merle's address or I would forward the letters and send addresses. Merle seemed to be needy for any letters, mine in particular. My sister, Betty, wrote him a long letter on a roll of toilet paper. He used that letter as a conversation piece for a long time after receiving it.

In one of his January letters, he wrote that he would keep my letters forever to make sure I kept the promises I made in those letters I wrote to him. He wrote of his love for me constantly and I did the same.

Dave's wife, my other sister, sent Merle a fruit cake and some nuts which he shared with his 74th Field Hospital team.

He wrote me many times in January that he cried when he received my letters. His letters to me made me cry as well. For some reason unbeknownst to either of us, Merle received a new APO number on January 17th. We suspected that it was meant to confuse any people from the enemy's side but never found out for sure.

Jan. 18, 1945
Darling Wife:
Hello Mommy. How is my Sweety tonite? I just came home from the show so I will write and tell you what is new for the day. The show was in technicolor and was pretty good. I don't know what the name was as I was a little late in getting there. After chow Johnson and I took a shower and shaved so that made us a little late getting to the show.

MERLE AND VALENTINA MARTIN

Technicolor was new to the both of us, so I did not know what he was talking about at the time. After the war ended, I learned by seeing a Technicolor movie for myself.

Wally and Velma were having problems. After being discharged because she enlisted underage when the two were married at Camp Pickett, Velma rejoined the WACs. Wally was feeling hurt and angry. Merle wrote about him being cool Johnson and him. Wally felt bad about his predicament. Neither Merle nor Wally liked the WACs or the Red Cross girls which was a typical expectation of the men in those days since women were still generally considered to be second class citizens. Wally visited with Merle about his predicament and with Gusler as well. Both Merle and Gus tried to make him feel better. Velma was sent to basic training in Georgia this same month.

Oh yes! Velma is joining the WACs again. Walley received a letter yesterday telling him so. He wrote her just a half of one page and told her things would be different from now on. He said he didn't care now whether she wrote often. It's really too bad and he has my sympathy. Just think him over here fighting for her and then her acting like that. Boy I know what would happen if I were in his shoes. I'm sure you won't do anything I ask you not to Honey you better not either.

I just took time out to listen to the ten o'clock news. By God old Hitler is really catching hell now and he is going to have to hollar Uncle before long if the Russians keep on like they have been. Won't that be the day mommy and then I can start looking for that boat to bring me back to you Darling. Gee won't that be swell Honey when I can come home and have nothing to do but smooch you and what I mean that's all I am going to do is smooch you and make you happy.

I received the cigarettes you sent me with that good old Iowa stamp on them. I just smoke them in the evenings and at special times. I don't know why they taste better than the Luckies I get here but they do even if the ones you sent me were mashed a little. I think that's why they taste better is because you sent them and it is really sweet of you to do things like that for a mean old husband like me. Even tho I am an old meany I can stand on a stack of bibles and say one thing and that is, "I am one-hundred per-cent true to my Sweet little Wife and I am really proud to be able to say that. It will never be different either Darling and I mean that from the bottom of my heart.

Gee I hope I get a letter from you tomorrow, I'm going to be terribly unhappy if I don't and I don't want to be any sadder than I am so please bring me a letter Honey. You will, won't you?

In Hawaii, Merle was still able to hear the Hit Parade on Saturday nights which had been our favorite pastime. He wrote me that he heard the song "Together" by Sammy Kaye as well as "I Walk Alone," and "Sweet and Lovely" and thought of me. We both liked Sammy Kaye.

I was hired (against Merle's wishes) by Rath Packing Company in the office in the order writing department and was responsible for orders to ship meat to APO numbers to servicemen overseas or wherever they were. We only used APO numbers, so most of the time, I did not know where the meat was going unless I recognized Merle's APO number instantly. I would be the only one to know it at Rath's. My pay was twenty-five dollars for forty hours each week plus overtime. Merle's earlier objections to my working at Rath's or Deere came from his own experience at the factory because he worked at Rath Packing Plant after high school. At least that's why I thought he didn't want me working there.

During another period of down time, my crafty husband built himself a foot locker so he would not have to live out of a barracks bag because he could never find anything when he did. Everything you needed was always at the bottom. After the war, he wrote that he would possibly build all of our furniture for our dream house that he suggested. He wrote, "Maybe I'll be a millionaire some day." The work ethic was sinking in.

I just heard the news and it sounds as if it won't be long until the Russians will be in Berlin and then things will be over in a hurry. Won't that be a great day Darling?

Front window of Rath Packing Company, where Val worked while Merle was overseas.

Merle and undoubtedly the rest of the 74th listened to the news constantly. News later in the month said the Russians were only one hundred and ninety miles from Berlin. The 74th was looking for the end of hostilities in Europe. I also listened to the news which seemed to break up occasionally so I was never sure whether it was good, bad, or propaganda.

On January 21st, Merle wrote that he, Gusler, and Johnson happened upon some food in their camp. Having nothing but C rations most of the time, the boys were always on the hunt for anything edible, especially fruit cocktail which—after Merle finally came home—he couldn't eat anymore since that seemed to be all they could find.

DEAR VALENTINA

Jan. 23, 1945
Darling Wife:

Hello Honey! How are you tonite? I hope well and just as sweet as ever. Today was a big day for me as I worked with the mail until about 9:30, then I got cleaned up to go to town and visit Pookey. I got to town O.K. but after I got there, I got lost and I got on the wrong bus three times before getting to the Navy Yard where he is at. After going thru all that trouble they wouldn't let me in as the marines are very strict So that made me mad and all I could do was leave. I went back down town and shopped for a few souveniers to send home to you. I bought you three handkerchiefs, a table scarf and a little mirror all of them have something about Hawaii on them. They don't amount to much but things are so terribly high that it is foolish to buy much. I am going to get you one of those Hawaiian blouses after pay day but couldn't afford it today. Anyway you will know I am thinking of you all the time. I also got Betty one of those little mirrors.

I came back here at 6:30 tonite all tired out and disgusted that I didn't get in to see Pookey again but yesterday when he was out to see me he said he would come back tomorrow if I didn't get out there.

After being all tired and mad I didn't get any mail from you today. Now my morale really is low. Some of the boys from New York have received word that their wives had gotten mail from them allready and the latest letter I have from you was written the eleventh. I wonder what is wrong Darling. Surely you are writing me regularly and it isn't as far from Iowa as it is from New York. I hope I get a half dozen letters from you tomorrow.

Today I did receive a swell box of Johnson's chocolates from my pal, Betty. They really tasted good as I've already sampled them. It said on the outside of the package "don't open till Xmas," so I am going to write Betty and ask her if she meant last Xmas or next one.

Tonite Walley come over and sit on my bed and we had a good talk. Velma left for the WAC's on the fifteenth and he is really disgusted. He asked me what he should do and I told him I wouldn't advise any one about those things, but he knew what I would do if it were me. I guess he is about thru and I don't blame him. It surely makes it tough for him and he has all my sympathy. I guess he is going to change his insurance and stop his allotments. Don't blame him a bit, do you. Personally she is no damn good and no one else acts that way. It shows they have no love or respect for their loved ones.

I found a nice leather folder in a Navy store today for your picture so hope they hurry up and get here. It is the same size of my billfold.

Honey I saw a foreigner driving a Buick convertible just like ours in town today and did it ever make me homesick for you. I really don't care if I never go to town again as there is no fun in it. If you were here, well we could see the scenery and enjoy it a lot but for me alone I'd rather stay in camp and sleep and write letters to you. When I see people riding around in cars enjoying theirselves, it makes me more lonesome than ever so I'm staying away.

Merle was also intending to do some mechanical work for Colonel Damron, but he was so upset about not being able to see Dave that he went straight to bed. Dave had been expecting Merle, but had promised that if Merle would not be able to get in—which he wasn't—Dave would return to see Merle the next day.

While he was repairing a refrigerator in the warehouse at Camp Koko Head the following day, "Pookey" showed up to Merle's surprise. He had received Merle's letter from the address I sent him. Dave was located at the Navy Yard on Hawaii. He told me that Merle's headquarters were much nicer than his at the Navy Yard and asked Merle to visit his quarters. The following day, Dave returned again, and went swimming with Merle near the beach, momentarily escaping the burdens of being soldiers for one afternoon. Merle and Dave visited a few times until Dave was on alert and left for parts unknown.

DEAR VALENTINA

Merle's special assignment for Colonel Damron was not as exciting or as dangerous as he would have thought. His duty was to install an aerial on the colonel's radio so they could get better reception on the island. Though it was a small task, it was a very important one because the men needed to hear the news of the war abroad.

All through the month of January, I felt lost as I tried to find my own self. I now needed to support myself alone for the first time. Although I had my family behind me, I was trying to be a reliable adult.

Merle was undergoing more training in jungle warfare in Hawaii. He did not give any details in his letters, but he did express his relief in a later letter in February when he wrote, "Yesterday we finished our jungle training and am I glad." It was without question a demanding and probably terrifying experience, but I think he knew that he was going to need the training.

About you working at Raths, well I guess it's O.K. as long as you go to work and then straight home and don't ever work at nite. You know how the people are that work there but you should be able to take care of yourself and not let anyone talk you into any foolish notions. I'm sure you won't. I know it pays good money working there but you must remember money isn't everything in this world.

About taking you abroad when this war is over is out as far as I am concerned. After seeing as much water as I have it will even be hard to get me in the bathtub. I'm sure I'll be content to sit out in front of our little bungalow in a lawn chair and talk sweet words to you. A trip down town for groceries will be far enough for me. Ha!

As for the gal you used to know in Hawaii just forget about it as I'm not interested, I am one of the few men who is really proud and loves his wife. I also don't care about the hula-hula. Regardless of how good things sound they don't bother me. I can't stop you from doing what you want to, but I can keep myself where I belong. By the way Honey what do you mean by even trying to put ideas in my head? You devil you.

Darling, there is one thing you can admire your old mean husband for and that is you never need to worry about him being true and sweet to you. After being with me for three years I think you've found that out for yourself. In case you haven't I'm telling you now, so don't ever forget it. It comes from the bottom of my heart. You just be the same way and we will be the sweetest and happiest couple in the world. I dreamt again last nite that I was home smooching the devil out of you. Gee, it seemed good to be back with you again. Honey hurry and stop this war so my dreams can come true. All I ask of this world is to be with you all the time and have every ounce of your love with all sincerity.

Just think, the sweetest and most beautiful wife, a little dream house built just to suit Mommy, and a big Buick. What more can a man ask for.

I have the most important part now and when I get back you and I together will get the rest, won't we Honey?

Gee Mommy I worship you from the top of your head to the tip of your toes. I suppose you get tired of hearing that over and over but I can't help it and want you to know and believe it.

Here's a big hug and a sweet kiss for you to sleep on Darling. Be a sweet mommy and pray for the war to end soon. Good-nite and God Bless you, Honey!

With all my love for my sweet Mommy I remain,
Yours Forever and Ever
Merle

FEBRUARY 1945

February found Merle still on beautiful Oahu, Hawaii, at Camp Koko Head with all the services the U.S. Army could provide. I was now working at a new job in the offices of the Rath Packing Company, earning my $25 for a full week of work. Merle remarked in one of his letters that it was "good money," but he warned me to avoid the bad influences of some of my co-workers. Rath was one of the largest meat-packing companies in the country during the war and a nationally well-known brand until the company closed in 1985. The company was shipping its products to the troops overseas in both the Pacific and European Theaters of War; the meat was sent to men by way of various American Post Office numbers. I was very much aware of this because I worked long hours in the offices there, many nights, five days a week; it was some comfort to me that I knew that I was doing something to help keep the troops fed particularly when I recognized Merle's APO number.

Feb. 1, 1945

I heard over the radio today that 500 American prisoners were captured from the Japs and they gave out their names, nine of them were from Iowa. We have a couple of artists in the outfit and they drew some V-Mail Valentines so I'm sending you and all our folks one. It will be something for your scrap-book.

Well, Pookey hasn't come back to see me so I guess you know what that means. You better tell Valeria not to get excited if she doesn't hear from him for a while. I don't believe he ever did write her as often as I do you, did he Honey? You can see that your poppa is really on the ball. He never misses writing his Darling Wife even tho he doesn't hear from her every day.

MERLE AND VALENTINA MARTIN

The news said today that the Russians were only 35 miles from Berlin on one front. It surely sounds good only if it's true.

I am sending you a coconut today and if you don't know how to open it, take it down to your Dad and he'll open it for you.

We had fresh eggs for breakfast this morning. They tasted pretty good. We've been used to eating powdered eggs, and I can't eat them. Last night over the 10:00 news broadcast, they said the Russians were only 58 miles from Berlin on one front. Sounds pretty good if they can keep it up. It can't be over too soon to suit me.

On February 1, 1945, the Joint Chiefs of Staff approved the final plans for the invasion of Okinawa, code name: "Operation: Iceberg." Of course, Merle's unit, the 74th Field Hospital was not aware at the time of its role in what was about to take place. In preparation, before all this took place, Merle was sent to "refrigerator school" with Gusler. He was still sending coconuts to me and various family members by mail at the low cost of 50 cents apiece. He recalled picking up a coconut for Colonel Damron, the eyes, ears, and throat doctor commanding his unit; Colonel Damron wanted one to send to his daughter back home in Tennessee. He also sent me various small gifts and postcards. I carefully kept all these little reminders of his love and devotion.

One of the boys sent his wife a grass skirt today but I'm not going to send you one until I can be there when you put it on.

Merle was depressed by reports of war that gave him the impression that he might be gone for another two years of duty. The war seemed so far away and hopeless to me even though Merle was in no immediate danger in beautiful Hawaii. I too was deeply saddened by his mention of the possibility of two years— and we had then been separated for only two months. No one knew what the future held though everyone was aware that more lives were about to be lost and more families shattered forever.

DEAR VALENTINA

All I could do was cry when I received his letters and wait and watch for more letters from my beloved husband. In the meantime, I buried myself in my job.

aloha
nui

all my love for you
Darling

Poster card sent to Val from Merle while stationed in Hawaii

Keep writing me lots of long letters like the one I got today and tell me all about yourself and everything that pertains to you. Here's a big hug and a sweet kiss for you. Good-nite, Darling and God Bless you. I'll always remain the same true Poppa to you so don't let me down Darling.
Yours Forever & Ever
Merle

Merle wanted me to have a Parker 51 fountain pen like the one I had given him before he left the United States. His reasoning, undoubtedly, was that I would use it to write him more often; his letters were filled with requests—sometimes petulant, which was quite understandable—for more mail. In fact, he often asked me only half-seriously, to spend all my spare time writing to him. At the same time, he insisted sincerely that he wanted me to be happy, safe, and healthy while he was away. I believe that Merle's failure to mention his own fear of self-sacrifice was probably common among troops who would serve on foreign soil. However, I still felt it.

On Febrary 4th, Merle wrote that he and Johnson infiltrated another outfit at lunchtime and had a turkey feast. He was so full that he felt like he was stowing away another turkey dinner when they left. A few days later, Walley received a letter from Velma that informed him that she was now undergoing basic training in Georgia. According to Merle, she was writing Walley regularly and complaining as usual.

Feb. 6, 1945

Honey, I wrote you in the first couple of letters how seasick I was and that I never wanted another motorboat ride even if it was free. I threw up everything. Even my G.I. socks. I didn't eat. Nothing was fit to eat, and I gagged every time I went near the kitchen. It was really "Hell" and I only want one more ride—back to the states! On top of being sick, I was so lonesome for you, and I knew I was getting further away from home, further away from you all the time. If I had to do it over again, I'd have jumped off at Waterloo and taken the consequences, but I kept saying to myself I've got to do it for my Darling wife's sake.

We had roast beef for supper tonight, but I was so hungry that I ate it and thought it was alright. After chow, we had mail call, and then I went to take a shower and shave. I washed my head and I used drene shampoo.

Despite his attempts at being civilized and clean, Merle wrote that he would have to re-learn how to use silverware because he and the boys had gotten used to eating out of their helmets.

Feb. 9, 1945
Darling Mommy:

Well, Honey, you have an awfully tired poppa tonite. I have been on the move since 5:00 this morning and had only one meal. I've driven about 250 miles and been all over the island. This was our last day of jungle training and it was a real one. The outfit doesn't come into camp until tomorrow nite but you know Johnson and I, we came in a day ahead of time. We will be all rested up by the time the rest of them get in. I think it will take most all day tomorrow for me to get all the dirt off me. We have really caught hell for a week. Well, so much for that.

On February 10th, Wally received a one-page letter from Velma who said that she was visiting Chattanooga on a three-day pass. Upset by this, Wally hurt his leg so that he could be out of commission for a while. He began recovering a couple days later. That was also Merle's last day of jungle training.

Feb. 11, 1945
Darling Wife:
Happy Birthday Honey! Did Santa bring you lots of presents? I hope so and I wish I were there to help you celebrate it. I surely hope I can celebrate your next birthday with you.

Well, Gusler is the father of a baby girl born on Feb. 9. They named her Mary Ann. He received the telegram yesterday. It was a straight cablegram and only took four hours for it to get it here from Virginia. It didn't say how his wife was but she must be getting along alright. He is a proud poppa now and everybody is calling him "Pop Gusler." He bought a case of beer and drank it himself. All the enjoyment he got out of that is the big head. He was treating all of us and when he asked me what I wanted I told him I'd take a jar of peanuts.

Yesterday I was driving up the road and my hat blew off so I stopped to pick it up and while walking after it, I saw a sea shell and thought I'd look for a few more while I was there. I spent about 30 minutes and found a handful of all different kinds. I'm going to send them to you, and if you don't want them, give them to your mother as she can put them in her fish bowl and I know she likes things like that.

MERLE AND VALENTINA MARTIN

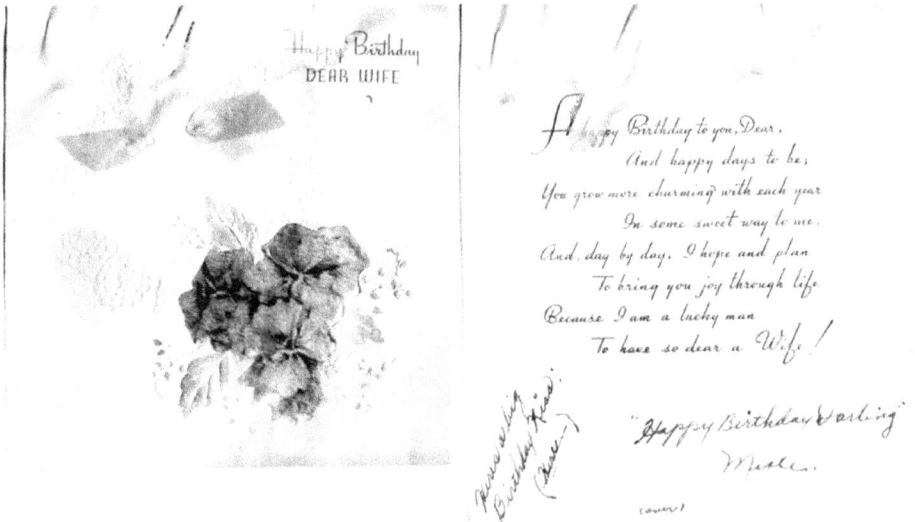

Birthday card sent to Val from Merle while stationed in Hawaii

The telegram informing Gusler that he was a father reached him in a mere four hours from Virginia which came as a surprise to Gusler and his close friends, all of whom were waiting in suspense with him for the birth of the baby at home.

My own birthday came on February 11th. Merle had sent his parents money to buy me a bouquet of red roses—a complete and wonderful surprise to me, yet Merle's sensitive nature and his concern for me were not at all surprising. He was constantly expressing his love for me and his devotion. His expression of sadness in being unable to share my birthday with me was obvious and sincere. Merle's love of flowers, especially red roses, of course, remained with him for all his life. On that day, however, Ray Bristow, an old friend of his from Waterloo, showed up. Naturally, Merle was delighted to see an old friend—especially one from his hometown. In the meantime, Valeria had not heard from Dave which we all feared meant that Dave was headed into battle.

Feb. 14, 1945
The news sounds good on all fronts, and I hope Germany surrenders soon. Then we can clean up Japan and come home.

34

DEAR VALENTINA

I'm sure sick of this damn war. I want to go home to you honey.
I miss you so much.

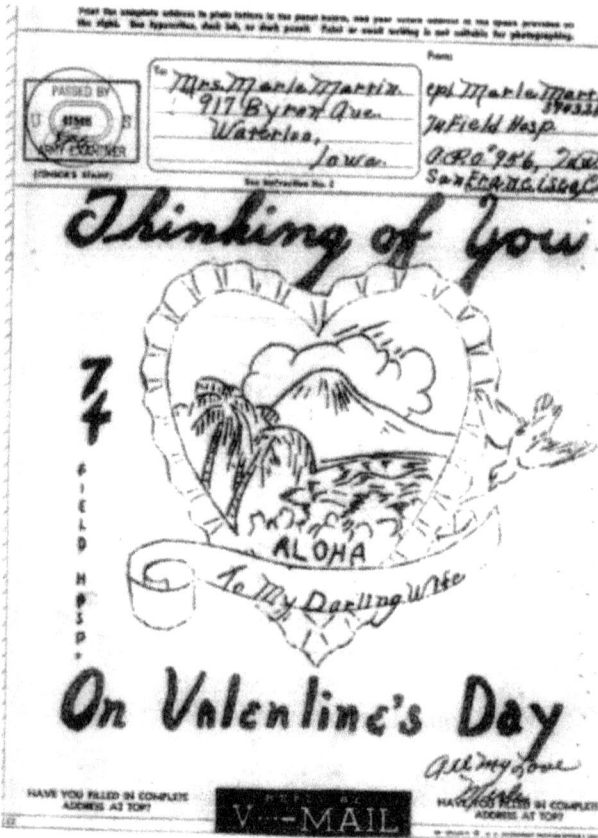

Valentines' Day Vmail sent to Val from Merle in Hawaii

In the middle of the month, Merle was expecting a promotion. In fact, he had talked to the colonel about it, telling him that his wife was counting on it. Later that year, sad news about Colonel Damron would reach Merle and the rest of the men, explaining why Merle never received that promotion.

The mailmen, Merle included since he was an assistant, were allowed to eat at the officers' mess hall once in a while because the food was so lousy at the field hospital.

MERLE AND VALENTINA MARTIN

On the 25th of February, a U.S. Army Air Force fleet of bombers struck Tokyo with incendiaries, and Merle heard about it while listening to the radio news broadcast in Hawaii. Good, accurate news was scarce for the servicemen, who followed the news intently because they knew that their futures depended upon the progress of the war.

Darling Wife:

Mommy I said I was going to write to you all afternoon but I didn't get any mail from you again today and I was so blue that I went to bed and stayed there until five-thirty. I was about half sick and blue too so I just stayed in bed. I ate supper and then Johnson and I had a game of checkers. After that I wrote to the folks. Now I'll write you what little news there is. You know after not hearing from you for four days, I don't have much to write about.

All I can do is tell you how much I love you. I'm sure if I keep telling you that too much you will get tired of it. Any way Mommy dear, my love for you will always be the same as long as you don't do anything wrong. As long as you stay sweet and true to me in every way, I'll love you with every ounce of my heart from the top of your head to the tip of your toes. I'm so lonely for you tonite, I don't know what to do. I've read the last letters I got from you over five times already and will probably read them again tomorrow. I can't figure out why I don't hear from you. All the rest of the boys get letters and I don't. Surely you are writing me aren't you Darling?

This morning Johnson and I finished the box of divinity candy you sent me. I put it on ice for a couple of days and it was really good.

I hope you receive the package I sent you soon because there is something in it that I know you will be glad to get it and also need too. You've been complaining about the old one every time you write me. I suppose you spent the week end at home again and know all the news of the week. Are they still drafting a lot of men or have they slowed down a little.

DEAR VALENTINA

Has Valeria heard from Dave recently? What does she do to pass her time anyway. I bet she stays home and counts her money every nite, doesn't she?

Wednesday is pay day for me again and am I glad. Even tho it won't be much it all helps. Gusler has just came from the show and is writing to his wife and new daughter and Johnson is playing checkers with one of the boys. Gusler says he expects a letter from his new daughter any day now. He is a pretty proud poppa.

I just heard the ten o'clock news and they bombed Tokyo again. It sure is terrible how the defense workers keep on striking. It seems as tho they don't want the war to end. I wish they would send every one that strikes overseas then maybe they would realize how it is to be away from home.

How much do you love your poppa tonite? Gee Honey I hope you love me as much as I love you because if you do you would never do anything wrong. I want to get home so bad so we can have a home of our own and start out where we left off at. I know this war can't last always so if we just be patient and keep looking forward to the day when we will be back together again. Then we will make up for lost time in all ways, won't we Honey.

Darling I can't think of any thing else to say so I'm going to kiss you and go to bed. I'm going to pray for you and that I receive lots of long and sweet letters from you tomorrow.

I know I haven't written much but I've told you the main thing which is how much I love you. If I get mail from you tomorrow, I'll really write you a long letter. I'll write you a Vmail in the morning.

Good nite and sweet dreams, my Darling. Here's a big hug and an awfully sweet kiss for you to sleep on. I hope and pray you will always stay faithful and true to me in every way even tho opportunity knocks once in a while. Write me when you have a spare moment. How about it Mommy?
Your Faithful Husband
Forever and Ever
Pa

MERLE AND VALENTINA MARTIN

"Good-nite and Sweet Dreams Darling"
P.S. I know I'm going to have sweet dreams about my mommy tonite. I'll tell you about them in the morning. You see, Darling, I spend all my time writing you. You do the same.

In Merle's letters to me, there was never any mention of fear for himself but only hopes for nothing to happen to me. I too in my letters mentioned it, although I was also concerned about him. Some of the letters I wrote him ended up in the East China Sea because of a typhoon later in 1945. Memories sixty-six years later still run deep. Fortunately, I wasn't the only person with the responsibility of keeping Merle's morale up. His nephews, Curtis and Mel were also writing him letters regularly, and he wrote back. Toward the end of the month, Valeria finally received a letter from Dave which he had written at sea. When Merle learned that Dave was at sea, he was almost positive that he and Dave were being sent to the same area.

On February 17, 1945, Merle received his Asiatic-Pacific ribbon,[4] knowing then that he was on his way to the Pacific. Whether he was headed north, south, east, or west remained a mystery for the time being. At the same time, the Russians were battering Germany to pieces from the east while U.S. and British armies pushed across the bombed-out country from the west. It was clear to Merle and his comrades in the 45th division in Europe that the war in Europe was coming to a close—cold comfort to thousands of us who knew that the men in Okinawa were yet about to face a vicious and determined enemy in the Pacific.

---

4   The Asiatic-Pacific ribbon is yellow with five narrow white stripes, three red stripes, and a single white one. It was created by an Executive Order of President Franklin D. Roosevelt, and its colors represented flags of both Japan and the United States. This service ribbon was issued to all members of the military who served in the Pacific Theater between December 7, 1941 and March 2, 1946. In 1947, the ribbon was converted to a regular campaign medal. Merle's term of service would have been completed by March of 1946.

MARCH 1945

March 3, 1945
To my Darling:

Honey you were very sweet to me today, you brought me two air mail letters. Boy, was I glad to hear from you. Your letters were written on Feb. 22 and 24. I wonder where the one of the 23rd is. You know I really like those ten page letters and wished you would write more of them.

Today was another busy day for me and I just finished taking a bath. It is now ten o'clock. I have carried the Star-Clipper around in my pocket for two days and still haven't found time to read it.

I got my watch all wrapped up and ready to send to you and also your grass skirt. Johnson and I went to the PX for a coke tonite and saw some Hawaiian compacts so decided to get you one. They have Air Core Insignia on them but that is all they had so guess you won't mind. I'm sending it tomorrow.

How does my mommy feel after another week's work? I'll bet you are tired and really in dream land by now. At least you better be. What are you dreaming about any way Honey? Tell me in your next letter and don't leave out a single part of it.

I'm glad you sent Gusler's wife a baby present. Her address is just Stuart, Va. She is getting along fine and says the baby is really growing.

I am sending my Easter cards and Mother's Day Greetings out so I'll have it over with, so if you receive them a little early don't open them until the right day. I am sending you a Mother's Day Greeting too Darling, even tho we don't have any children as yet because you are my sweet Mommy.

Merle and Valentina Martin

By the sound of your letters you must really be having winter back home. Gee, Mommy, I wished I were there to keep you warm. Boy would we do some old fashioned loving.

I'd surely like to know where Pookey was, of course I have a good idea same as you. The Marines are rough and he'll probably see plenty before he gets back. I don't know what to think about this damn war, sometimes I don't think it will ever end, altho things seem to be going pretty good in Germany. All we can do is hope and pray it will end soon so we can be back together again. It has been going nearly three and a half years now so it surely won't last much longer. Pray every nite, Darling, so we can build that little dream house.

I surely hope I get your other picture pretty soon so I can love it and smooch the devil out of it. I'm going to have this other one loved to pieces before long.

At the beginning of March, I sent Merle a letter with a clipping with Toy's hair. Our dog wanted Merle to know what he missed him just as much as I did, and I wanted to make sure Merle had something to remember him by. Merle got a good laugh out of Toy's token of love.

March 4, 1945

Johnson and I went over to chow, but all they had to eat was sauerkraut and wieners, so we went over to the PX for an ice cream and candy bars for supper.

Don't buy bonds, darling. If you have any extra money, put it in your account. Over here, our job is winning, and the ones back home can buy the bonds.

Merle was busy sending Easter Cards and Mothers' Day cards well ahead of time to ensure that they would arrive on time. His concern for his close friend and brother-in-law, "Pookey," was very much on his mind too. The change of Merle's APO was another clear indication that he would soon be leaving Hawaii. After nine weeks in Hawaii, Merle and the 74th Field

Hospital were given notice of their potential departure date—March 5th or 6th.

```
March 5, 1945
Notice of Change of Address
This is to notify you that my current address
is:
cpl. Merle R. Martin 37432596
74th Field Hospital
APO No. 331 c/o Postmaster San Francisco, Calif

Signature
```
Merle R. Martin

```
Important: No message or other information will
be entered on this form.
```

While Merle and Johnson were busy sending out their address change cards, two boys from the post office were informed that they would be able to go home on furlough. Those two soldiers had been away from home for 27 months. Merle wrote that he would die before he stayed away from home that long.

They were scheduled to depart on the 15th of the month. Supplies and equipment were loaded onto the *U.S.S. Okanogan*. The cooks and kitchen personnel boarded that ship too before the rest of the troops. Truck drivers left, including Ralph Byers and Merle's friend Weaver on the *U.S.S. Valencia*, while the rest of the outfit was aboard the *U.S.S. Okanogan*. On the 15th, the unit sailed away from Hawaii toward a destination still unknown to them. Merle left Camp Koko Head, steaming out of Honolulu Harbor on the *U.S.S. Okanogan*. By March 10th, Merle had undoubtedly been notified that he would be leaving for parts unknown.

Don't worry if you don't hear from me for a while.

MERLE AND VALENTINA MARTIN

He spoke of last-minute shopping and of shipping items home, including the grass skirt that he was going to bring. Memories of Camp Pickett also began to appear.

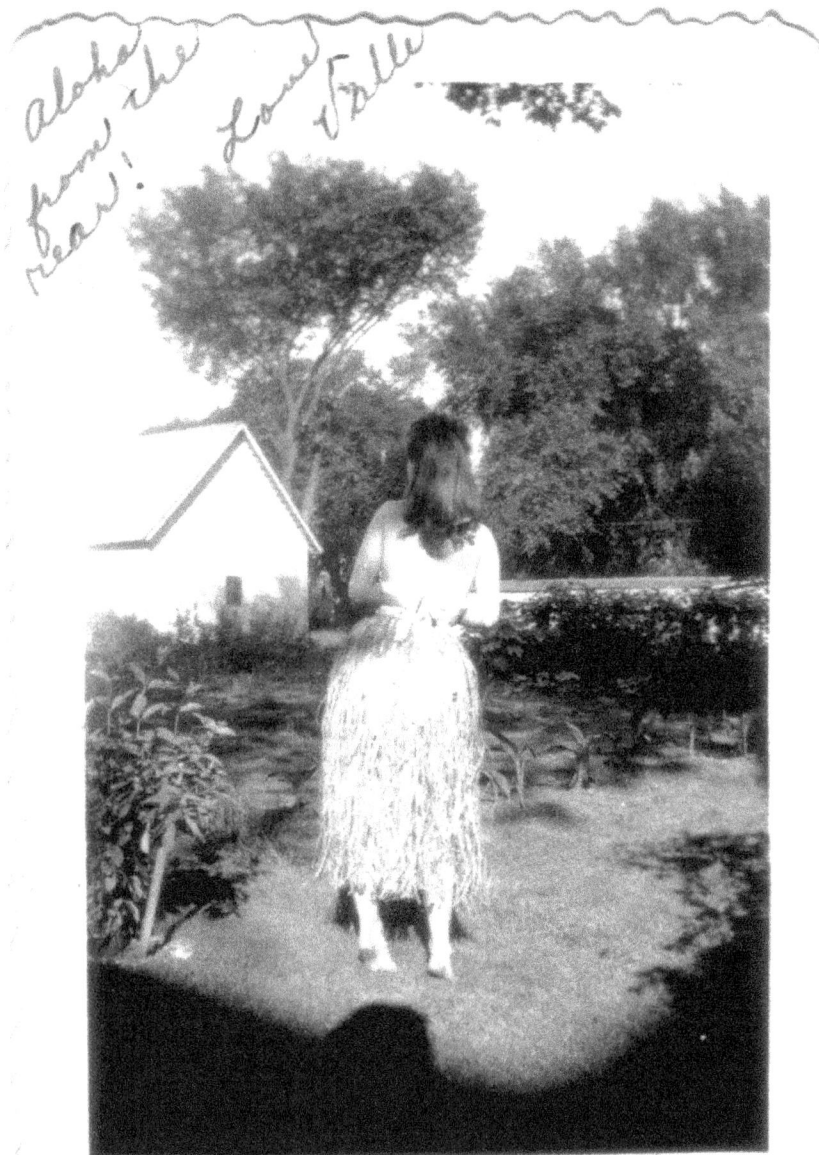

Val modeling the Hawaiian grass skirt for Merle.

Dear Valentina

I received a nice Easter greeting from Valeria today, she wrote a line telling me that Dave is in Iwo Jima with the 3rd Division. I hope and pray he will come out alright. I must write her a line tonite and thank her for the card. I also got a letter from Curtis. I guess he is just as devilish as he used to be

I should get the little picture and folder tomorrow if you sent it air mail because I got your letter of the 24th yesterday. I want it so I can carry it in my left pocket right over my heart all the time then I can kiss you every five minutes if I want to. How would you like to have me to kiss you every five minutes Darling? I bet you wouldn't care, would you? That 5 x 7 picture of you is absolutely perfect. I look at it every nite and kiss it before I go to bed and always have to shed a few tears.

You should be getting your pen any day now. It is wrapped good in the box that the pillow top is in. I'm sure you will like it because money won't buy a better one. When you get it I want you to sit down and write me a thirty page letter. Now don't forget it Darling. As for the cigarette lighter you sent me I'm going to keep it. I wouldn't sell it at any price because you gave it to me. If I lose my one of my other lighters I will need it. Yes, Darling, you know I still have the lighter you gave me. It works perfect only in the wind it's not so good.

Why shouldn't I show your picture to every one? It is the prettiest picture any woman has ever taken and I'm so proud of it that I'm going to show it to everyone whether you like it or not. Now I'm pouting, Mommy! Ha! Don't ever let me hear you say anything like you did about your face again. It makes me feel bad because I know you are wrong, you know you have a nice looking face and the sweetest one in the world. You never need to worry about my loving you always, Darling, because I couldn't love you any more if I tried.

Honey I'm glad you had a nice time at Marvin's party. God I wished I could have been there with you. Then I know we both could have had a good time. Why did you have to talk about that good pumpkin pie, you know how I like pie and especially if you made it. I'll never forget those good meals you prepared for me when we had that little apartment in Macomb.

MERLE AND VALENTINA MARTIN

I surely wish we were there now or any place just so we could be together.

After Merle left the harbor, the parts unknown remained unknown. For the first days, the seascape was extremely interesting to a landlubber like him, but it soon lost its fascination, especially when the sea grew rough. Ice cream became the main attraction during those days and nights when the seemingly endless waves got high. The men standing in a long line to buy a pint of ice cream found the wait to be hot and extremely tedious, but for Merle, it was worth the effort. None of the soldiers had much to do, so they did not mind. He wrote at one point of going through the line twice, despite the fact that this required hours of standing in line.

At Sea
To my Darling:
Hello Mommy dear! How is every thing back home by now? I am on guard now for a few days, four hours at a time and does the time ever pass slow. Last nite I was sitting up on deck and was it ever a pretty nite, a full moon and just as light as day. I kept looking at it and thinking how you and I used to sit out under the moon, then I had to cry. Gee Honey if they don't bring me a letter from you soon I'll go crazy. I'm so lonesome for you and don't know if you are well or not. I worry about you more each day so you can see you'll have a gray-haired poppa when he gets back. If I could only get a letter from you it would help so much and I would at least know if you were safe and well.

How much does momma love poppa today? I hope you are as lonesome as I am so you will know exactly how I feel. Are you having sweet dreams about me every nite like I am you? I hope so Darling because I love you with every little ounce of my heart, I want to be with you so bad. This war is really bad for us fellows who have loved ones and families home waiting for them, isn't it? Let's hope and pray that it ends soon so we can be together again. I want to have a home of our own so bad. Just think we've been married over three years and both of us have had to live out of a suit case or barracks bag most of the time. Boy when I get out of this damn mess no one will ever get me out of your sight. I want you to be with me in every single move I make. Will that suit you Honey?

How is every-thing at the office by now. Have you had any more arguments with the gals? Don't let them tell you any thing Mommy, if they get smart put them in their place. I'll back you up. I haven't written any of the folks because there is so little to talk about and besides I have a hard time writing on my knee so you can tell all of them hello for me and that I'm O.K. only lonesome for my sweet mommy. You know Honey I wouldn't mind this trip at all if you were here. We have pretty good chow and fairly clean bunks only it gets pretty tiresome sleeping on a strip of canvas and it is terribly hot all the time. I suppose by now you've received the watch, pen and all the souveniers. I'm looking forward to that twenty-page letter that you promised me as soon as you receive the pen.

I hate it so bad that I didn't get that little picture and folder of you before I left because God knows when I'll get it now. I have the large one of you under my blanket and I sleep with it every nite. That is really a sweet picture of you Darling, and even Toy looks so real. Every time I look at it I get so down-hearted and so mad at this war.

On March 19th, the *U.S.S. Okanogan* crossed the International Date Line, so for them, March 18th did not exist. On March 21st, the *U.S.S. Okanogan* experienced eight hours of rough seas. Luckily on the 23rd, the ship arrived at the Eniwetok Atoll in the Marshall Islands.[5] Eniwetok's area is a mere 2.25

---

[5] On February 17, 1944, an assault force of U.S. Marines and Army troops under the command of Adm. Richmond Kelly turner invaded Eniwetok. Six days of air strikes, naval gunfire, and artillery supported the ground troops who took control of the atoll with a loss of only 195 men. The Japanese forces were completely destroyed; a mere 64 men of the original 2,700 Imperial Japanese forces survived. Eniwetok was subsequently used as an airbase for the "island hopping" campaign that won the Pacific War for the American Forces. Later, Eniwetok was used as a testing ground

square miles of sand, approximately 50 miles in circumference, surrounding a lagoon.

VMail
At Sea
Sweetheart:

 Good Morning, Darling! I wrote you a five page air mail letter last nite but thought I'd drop you a few lines this morning to say Hello and tell you how much I love you. I want you to get lots of mail even if I can't

 Gee, I had a sweet dream about you last nite. It sounded so real that I could almost see you sitting by my side. You are so sweet. I love you so much, Mommy Dear. I am the proudest husband in the world. Please keep me that way always by staying true and faithful to me in every single way.

 Here's a great big kiss for you, Darling. I'll write you another letter tonite. Don't forget I love you with my heart, body and soul. I'll always remain "Yours Darling"
Forever & Ever
Merle

At Sea
To my Darling:

 Good Morning, Honey! I'll bet you are still in bed because it is four o'clock and I'm on guard again. Thank God I only have one more day of it because I'm really tired. Are you having sweet dreams about me? I hope so Darling because I always do about you. This morning I was in the middle of a nice dream when they woke me up. It made me mad because I wanted to finish it. Boy, is it ever hot. I never sweat as much in all my life as I have since we left Hawaii. We take salt tablets because we sweat so much. What I wouldn't give to see a little of that good Iowa snow.

---

for atomic weapons research. The U.S. Government changed the official spelling to *Eniwetok* in 1974 to reflect the native population's pronunciation of the name.

Dear Valentina

I am on guard on one side of the mess hall and Johnson on the other and believe me we are really doing some cussing about this damn war. Guess it doesn't do any good but it makes us feel a little better anyway. He is writing his wife too. I sure wished this war was over so all the boys could go home to their loved ones. It isn't so bad for a fellow if he isn't married but it is really tough on a married man especially if he has a sweet wife waiting for him like I do.

Gee, Mommy, I'm so lonesome for you that I'm about crazy. I've been in an ugly mood for sometime now because I haven't received one letter from you and believe me, no one better argue with me because I'm really in a fighting mood if I ever was. Remember how I used to be when I was tired, well that's not half as bad as I am now. Don't get worried, Darling, because all it would take to make me happy and cheerful again is to see you and it would help a lot even if I could get a few letters from you. I have read the old ones over and over and I believe I have them all memorized by now but I still enjoy reading them. I just try to make myself believe they were written yesterday and they tell me what I love to hear which is how much you love me. I hope that your love for me will never die, Darling, because all I live for is you and without you there would not be any fun in living. See Mommy Dear that is how much I love you and worship you with every ounce of my heart so please don't ever do anything wrong and always stay true and faithful to me in every way. We are missing out on a lot of living now but will make up for all of it when I get back, won't we Honey? Just think, Mommy, when we get our little home and a nice car out in front all shined up. What more could we ask for. To me that is something really worth fighting for and besides I know it will please you too because you've always wanted a nice home. As yet I haven't gotten my promotion but expect it soon. Any way I better get it or they will hear about it. I'd surely like to know if Pookey is well and safe. I can imagine just how Valeria feels. How are all the folks? Tell them hello for me and not to worry about me. Just take good care of you until I get home. I'll bring the Tokyo Rose with me. Ha!

You should see Gusler he has his hair cut within a half inch of his scalp and with his long nose he really looks funny. How many hours are you working a week? I don't want you to put in over 50 because if you did, there wouldn't be enough time for you to write me and still get your rest. You can't get rich in a minute so don't overdo.

Tell your Daddy he should be here to play poker with us. That is all we do in our spare time. I'm ahead for the trip and most of the boys are broke so we've dropped the limit from a quarter to a nickel. I've made enough to buy you a nice suit so I'm doing O.K., don't you think so Honey? I can't think of anymore to say so will close for now with every ounce of my love for you Darling. Always stay a sweet and true mommy to poppa in every way so he can be the proudest husband. Here's a big hug and lots of sweet kisses for the sweetest girl in the world, "You Darling". I'll always remain your faithful husband —

Forever & Ever
Merle
P.S. I hope you can read this. Here's another kiss for you Mommy Dear. Be a sweet Mommy to poppa always and write me lots of those personal letters telling me how much you love me and how true you will always be to me.

All the men were eager to get off the ship and explore the first land they had seen in weeks, but only about half the men of the 74th Field Hospital were allowed to join the first shore party to enjoy beer, Coca-Cola, and other refreshments away from the crowded, pitching, rolling ship. Higgins boats—flat-bottom boats meant to carry personnel to and from land—were moored at a crowded wharf; nearby, grateful military men stood around drinking beer in the shade. Most of these servicemen were—like the men of the 74th—just passing through on their way to a dangerous, unknown environment. Unfortunately for the other 50% of the men on the *U.S.S. Okanogan*, the ship had to depart before the last group got their chance to go ashore. Merle was writing to me early in the morning of the ship's sailing on March 26th.

On March 25th, there was great excitement among the troops as rockets and flares blazed in the sky, announcing the end of the war in Europe. This celebration turned out to be premature and was a false alarm. The war-weary men were too quick in their desire to see if an end of war was in sight, and they soon discovered that they had been fooled by a rumor. On March 26th, the 74th Field Hospital set sail from Eniwetok at 8:00 AM.

Merle's stay at Hawaii was about to end and of course because of 1945's snail mail, I was usually ten days behind while he was in Hawaii. Whenever he did write, I was not privy to the information since all his mail was censored. I continued to work at Rath Packing Company writing orders for meat for the U.S. forces all over the world to their American Postal Service numbers. There was a lot of overtime involved. Many nights I worked until 10:00 PM, and I did not have the time to write Merle the long letters he wanted. Those were long days, made even longer by my concern for Merle.

News from Europe was reporting that the Russians were only twenty-two miles from Berlin. We both hoped the war in Europe was ending. Merle being in Hawaii was a relief temporarily for me. He was basking in the sun, becoming more tan, and eating well.

APRIL 1945

April 1, 1945, "Love Day," as the invasion planners had designated it, was not only Easter Sunday but April Fool's Day as well. The American forces—with some support from the British Navy—began the assault on Okinawa with an armada of some 1,250 ships (some sources claim 1,500) of all kinds lying off the Okinawa shore—battleships, destroyers, and smaller warships shelled the island for days prior to the Love Day landing of troops, both Army and Marines, in order to make the landings as safe as possible for the infantry and artillery units—and the medical units as well who were always in danger. Merle landed on Ulithi Atoll on April 1st. The enormous lagoon there provided a harbor for the vast fleet taking part in the attack. As before at Eniwetok, the men of the *U.S.S. Okanogan* had to wait for several days offshore on the ship. Once they were able to go ashore, the men of the 74th Field Hospital rode around the lush green atoll in the plywood Higgins boats that would carry the troops to the beachheads. As a result, they began to understand just how valuable these crafts would be for the assault.

The *Okanogan* had a boat drill in preparation for the landing on April 2nd. On Easter Sunday, many soldiers from the *Okanogan* took a tour of Ulithi on the Higgins boats where they saw the native population. Ulithi Atoll had a large harbor, so many ships of the United States stopped there. Then they went back to their craps games. Merle said he won some money. He was happy since he had boarded the boat completely broke. I do not believe he realized how close to danger they really were at the time.

DEAR VALENTINA

At Sea
To my Sweetheart:
    Good Morning, Honey! How is everything with you today? I suppose you are hard at work now seeing how many hours you can get in this week and here I am sitting on my bunk writing to you. That is where I've been spending most of my time lately because I'm not on any details this week. Of course, I play a little poker every day. Yesterday, I got a little lucky and won a few dollars so I'm quite a little ahead this trip. I got on the boat practically broke so it helped quite a bit. I'll send you a little present as soon as possible.

    On April 9th, while still waiting aboard the *Okanogan* at Ulithi, the mascot of the 74th, a dog named Nina, jumped into a hatch and landed on the floor of the ship's mess hall. All the soldiers were very worried about how badly Nina had been hurt. Fortunately, after an exam by the ship's surgeon, they were informed that she sustained no serious injury. For these men about to go into mortal danger, the doctor's report came as a great comfort.

    At long last, on April 11th, the men were given their orders and briefed on their mission. They were also given information about the other islands in the Ryukyu group, of which Okinawa is a part. Merle's unit learned that they were to land on "Yellow Beach," the code name during Operation Iceberg for a stretch of sandy coast on the western side of the island. Their mission was to set up their field hospital not far from the beach—only about 1,200 yards from the vicious fighting on the front lines. It is important to note that the battleship's biggest rifles were capable of hurling an explosive shell the size of a car a distance of some 20 miles. Moreover, the Japanese forces on Okinawa were very well-equipped with first-rate artillery weapons of similar power and range. As a result—and Merle makes an indirect reference to this terrible danger—the men of the 74th could hear the terrifying sounds of shells from both opposing forces streaking through the air above them day and night.

MERLE AND VALENTINA MARTIN

In the midst of all the terror and suffering that afflicted these soldiers, the news of President Roosevelt's death on April 12th came as an awful blow, and it affected millions of peace-loving people all over the world in the same way. Newsreel footage taken at the time of his death and during his funeral shows crowds of weeping men and women. On that night, Merle attended a memorial service for the President; troops observed three minutes of silence in his honor.

An unfortunate delay of a mere 45 minutes hampered the work of Merle's unit when the *Okanogan* broke down. Consequently, the convoy that the ship was supposed to join had to take to sea without the *Okanogan*. Two destroyers were detailed to protect it from the Japanese submarines that were a constant menace during the Pacific campaigns; they picked on warships, supply ships, and troop transports.

The chilling sounds of distant artillery firing could be heard on April 17th as Merle and his comrades boarded the Higgins boats in the South China Sea, its glassy smooth surface a strange contrast to the sounds of murderous violence toward which they were heading. Upon landing, the unit was directed to the medical concentration area, a barren, desolate spot only a short distance from the beachhead. Then they simply had to remain in place, awaiting further orders to move up and establish their field hospital. They immediately dug a slit trench for protection—a necessity for that first night ashore. Japanese artillery, air attacks, and infiltrators were a constant threat. The slit trench was used that first night when an enemy fighter flew over the men and strafed them. No one was hurt, but it was a sobering introduction to what the men could expect to encounter from the very beginning of their experience on Okinawa.

As the men boarded the Higgins boats to take them to shore, they were surprised that there was little or no fighting to be seen, despite the rumble of heavy artillery and the pall of smoke hovering over the island. They did not expect to endure a storm of bullets as American troops had cleared the area before they landed. Many of the Higgins boats stopped well short of the beach, and thus they were unable to disembark directly onto dry land. They waded ashore in combat uniform, burdened with full field-packs through about two feet of sea-water until they were stopped by an underwater obstruction. They watched the "Water Buffaloes"[6]—large landing crafts—bringing in their tons of supplies. When they were finally given the signal, they grabbed their duffel-bags and headed inland for about 100 yards. Once there, they simply dropped all their gear in a pile and dined on "C" and "K" rations.

In two hours, they had a wonderful surprise: after weeks of no mail, there were bags full. Their plight seemed better because they received news from home. A mile down the newly-created dirt road at the medical concentration area, they began to dig in for the night. From their position there, they could see landing ships of various kinds moving supplies, often swerving to pass around wrecked U.S. Tanks and equipment. About mid-afternoon, a Water Buffalo ran over a hand-grenade which created quite an explosion, and the men ran over to investigate.

That night, the men got their first impression of what real combat was going to be like. A Japanese plane flew over and strafed their area—blasting away with machine guns. They were at the bottom of their trenches and could hear the deadly bullets striking around them. That taught them that their trenches were not yet deep enough. The low droning of the engines and the flames from the plane's exhaust pipes seemed very close and terrifying. They were in and out of those trenches all night. Air-raid sirens would wail, and suddenly they'd be in their trenches again.

In one of the letters, Merle mentioned that his friend Weaver was his roommate, noting that they kept their carbines loaded when they were in their foxhole. After a sleepless night listening to "Washing Machine Charlie,"[7] they were worn out, but they prepared to move up to the front of their hospital in the morning. So much for their first night on Okinawa—they knew

---

6 "Water Buffalo" was the unofficial name given the LVT(2) Landing Vehicle, Tracked, Unarmored (Mark II).

7 Nicknamed for the Japanese plane that flew over the encampment every night to bomb and strafe the landing forces.

their jobs and went on with them and helped out each unit as needed. Once they reached the designated area, they dug in again with the sounds of enormous artillery shells flying overhead from both U.S. Navy guns and Japanese guns.

The Marines and Army infantry had already cut the island in half and were spreading out to both the north and south. The Japanese offensive had already slowed down a few days. The 74th moved farther forward as the enemy began to put up stiffer resistance. They expected that it would be fierce and that the battle for the island would be costly in lives and equipment. Soon a truck came along to carry the men to the east side of the narrow island; it took them to a position only a short distance from a large bay that would be named for the commander of the land forces—General Simon Bolivar Buckner. Buckner, the highest-ranking officer to be killed in action during the war, was killed by a Japanese artillery shell on June 18, 1945 while in a forward position, observing the action of his troops.

When the men first arrived in the area, there was only a truck, a tent, and a few men from a mechanical unit who had been assigned to them as guards. Their presence—because everyone was now very much aware of how much danger they were in—was a real comfort to the soldiers. They put up their tents, dug slit trenches, and prepared to stay a while. On that first afternoon, they got their first sight of the "gooks," the derogatory name used by U.S. Forces for both the native Okinawans and Japanese natives.[8] They followed a road along the shore from the vicinity of the front lines, heading for a concentration area set up for them by the U.S. Military Government. These people had been forced out of the raging battle from their humble dwellings to retire to a rear-echelon area.

Merle's first few nights on the island were not pleasant. They were indeed, literally spending their nights on the island, sleeping on the ground with nothing under or over them. All of

---

8   The rather impoverished natives of the island, a prefecture of Japan, were culturally and linguistically related to the people of the home islands but were considered their inferiors.

the time they had spent upon arrival was devoted to setting up the field hospital. By the time the sunlight had all been spent, the men had not yet been able to set up their own tents.

On the 19th of April, a dugout resembling a log cabin was sunk into the ground for Colonel Damron's command post. The rain began to fall in torrents on that first night in the new camp. The men had been aware that it was the rainy season, but weren't prepared for the volume of rain that fell that first night. The rain washed out tent-poles and pegs and caused drainage ditches to overflow into the tents. One soldier had pitched his tent over his slit trench for convenience. On this day too, Merle received the terrible news that his friend and brother-in-law, Dave had been killed fighting with his Marine unit on Iwo Jima on March 3, 1945.

April 19
Sweetheart:

Hello Darling! How is my sweet Mommy tonite? It is nearly dark but I'll try to write you a few lines. My pen is out of ink so have to use pencil.

I received six sweet letters from you the day before yesterday and they made me so happy. They were written from the 24th to the 30th. I guess I'm still missing a few old ones. Yesterday I got three more from you and in the one you wrote the nite of April 1st told me the sad news about Dave. That is terrible. I went to the Chaplain to see about sending Valeria a message but he said conditions would not permit it. I surely feel sorry for her and she has my deepest sympathy. If there was anything I could do for her you know I would Darling. I don't know why but every day while I was on the boat I used to think about him because when we heard the news they would tell of the many casualties. It makes it so bad for Valeria, just think they hadn't been married a year yet. I think it is a blessing that they didn't have a baby on the way. I'm anxious to get the letter you wrote on March 31 so I will know if he is really dead or missing in action.

MERLE AND VALENTINA MARTIN

Things are really rough where they are at. The Japs wake us up every nite and we have to jump in our fox holes. I don't mind it though I want to do all I can to get this war over in a hurry so I can come home to you, Mommy Dear.

Yesterday I fell and hurt my leg so I can hardly get around this morning. We cannot say where we are except that we are north of the equator and have passed the International date line.

At dawn, Merle discovered himself, his tent, and his blankets, along with a few gallons of water, in a neighboring tent. They had to stay in the middle of all the tents. The canvas was so saturated that if someone touched one side of the tent, it would break. The men were curious about the condition of those standing guard during the rain storm and whether they'd managed to somehow stay dry. The guards had been wracking their nerves all night by firing wildly at things both seen and imagined. Everyone's nerves were stretched tight, but when the soldiers thought about their comrades on the front lines, they realized that they were very fortunate.

Today was another busy day for me and besides it rained again so the mud was belly deep. My legs are so tired that I can hardly move. I hope someday that I'll get caught up with my work so I can sit down and write you a long letter. About all I have time to write is to say Hello and tell you how much I love you. Of course that is the main thing.

On the following day, supplies were coming in, though the enormous amounts of mud created terrific difficulties. Supplies were covered with tarps, and vehicles cut deep ruts in the muddy Okinawa soil as they brought food, ammunition, weapons, medical supplies, and more from the beach to points across the island. The mud clung to their boots and made walking almost impossible. By the 21st, the medical tents were being set up, and they continued to make progress. Air-raid sirens blasted warnings day and night. From their position, the men could see planes being shot down as "AA" (anti-aircraft) guns from the ships nearby hit them with deadly flack bursts, creating great puffs of black smoke above them. Sometimes, the men ran for their slit trenches, but they usually just kept on working. At night, during an air-raid, the skies would be lit up in a display of pyrotechnics which would have delighted the kids at home on the Fourth of July. It was all very colorful, exciting, and deadly with sirens moaning and AA shells exploding. Machine guns created flashing chains of red with tracer bullets tracking their targets and powerful searchlights stabbed the sky, searching for enemy planes droning above.

Smack! Here's a big kiss Darling before you read this!
To my Sweetheart:

Hello my darling, how are you tonite? It has been raining all day and I was mud from head to foot tonite. If you think it gets muddy back home you should be here. After eating what I could find, I proceeded to wash up a little. It doesn't help much, but at least I feel better for awhile. It is ten o'clock now and I have to stay up until midnite to keep the generators running so I'll spend these two hours writing to you.

Gee Darling you can't imagine how hard we've been working, day and night and hardly time to smoke. On top of that we have had nothing but C Rations to eat. I smuggled a few cans of fruit along with me or I believe I'd have starved. Johnson and I brought thirty cartons of cigarettes and a lot of candy so I guess we will live.

Honey you didn't bring me any mail today so my morale is pretty low. Maybe I'll get some tomorrow. Any way I hope so because your sweet letters are all that keep me going from day to day.

Gee Darling I love you so much and am so proud of you. I only hope this damn war ends pretty soon so we can be back together again. Honey it seems like ages since we were together last. I'm so lonesome for you that I am about crazy. How much does momma love poppa tonite? I hope it is with every ounce of your heart because that is the way I love you Darling. Just so you stay sweet and true to me in every way and I'll do the rest. This war can't last always and when it does end, Oh Baby! will we make love. Well make up for all lost time in all ways, won't we Honey?

Johnson is sitting here trying to figure out where to put all his stuff. He sure is a good old pal to me. Between the two of us we will get along somehow.

The field hospital was set up and ready to go on the 26th when they treated their first patient, Private Woodrow W. Blair of the U.S. Army Second Division, 32nd Infantry. They had created a composite pattern of ward tents and individual personnel tents; they also established a Red Cross headquarters tent by joining two tents together. The engineers had graded a network of simple roads through the area. These were hardly more than wide walkways which formed a large horseshoe shape. More troops joined the main island roads and enclosed the hospital. On April 28th, a Red Cross worker, Bill Hubbard, from the 27th Division Station Hospital joined the unit.

All sections went into operation that day with the admittance of the first patient. It was the beginning of a long, weary grind that taxed the stamina of every man for many weeks. The first patients began to come in great numbers; handling them with the necessary skill, and doing it as swiftly as possible was a major job that required everyone to exercise the greatest care at every moment. That was the work that they had been trained to do, and they had learned those lessons well. The battle for Okinawa was characterized by horrific violence and brutality. The battle raged on as if it would never end, and casualties poured in. An endless unvarying routine even for highly-trained men improved their skills, efficiency, and endurance. The 74th was very much a part of this terrible battle, but their enemy was death, not men.

By the 29th, the U.S. forces were pushing the enemy toward the south end of the island. As they moved to keep close to the front, Merle's unit was gradually falling farther behind the lines compared with their first position, only about 1,200 yards away from the fighting. Air-raids continued day and night, usually caused by a single fighter plane that had managed to get through the storm of AA from the ground and from ships. By the end of the month, several ward tents had been set up to the west of the patients' tents in anticipation of the arrival of nurses. Their presence would undoubtedly raise the morale of the men in the unit. Reverend Runion, the Chaplain, had an office there in the compound. At the end of the month, Merle went to him to see whether he could send a sympathy message to his widowed sister-in-law, but conditions would still not permit it.

Merle with some of Val's letters.

MERLE AND VALENTINA MARTIN

April 23, 1945
To my Darling:

Hello Honey! How is my sweet Mommy tonite? I just finished my supper so will write you a few lines before it gets dark. I am really tired tonite and still have more work to do before I go to bed.

Weaver and I have our pup tent pitched together and we have a fox hole right beside it. When there is an air raid we can jump in it. Mommy this is a rugged life, if you could see how tough I look now you would probably disown me. The weather is pretty nice here only it gets really cool at nite, and the mosquitoes bite like hell.

I ransacked an old [censored] village today and got some hand painted dishes and a [censored] teapot. They are really nice and I'll send them home as soon as they will let me. We captured a milk cow and a couple of horses already and I have a couple of pigs spotted for a roast one of these days. You should see Weaver and I at nite we sleep with our guns loaded. Every time we hear a noise we are both ready to shoot. Johnson, Walley and Gusler all said to tell you Hello! We are all so busy that we hardly have time to talk. I haven't received any mail from you for two days but expect some tomorrow. Anyway I better get some because my morale is getting pretty low and I'm terribly lonesome for my sweet Mommy. Gee Honey if you only knew how much I loved and missed you. How much do you love me tonite? Are you having sweet dreams about me every nite? I never miss dreaming about you every nite and they are always sweet ones too. You little Darling you! In the day time I'm thinking of you every minute and wondering if you are well and what you are doing. Are you writing me every nite? Please do, Darling because your letters are all that keep me going.

I surely feel sorry for Valeria. I keep thinking about Dave and I can't believe that he is really gone. I hope somehow he isn't. He was such a swell guy and they made a good couple. I will try to find time to write our folks tomorrow but tell them all Hello anyway.

DEAR VALENTINA

Darling it is getting dark so I'll have to close for tonite. I'll write again tomorrow. Here's a big hug and lots of kisses for you Darling. I hope and pray you are well and safe. God Bless you Darling! Always stay a sweet and true wife to me in every way because I'll always remain, your faithful husband,
Forever & Ever
Merle

MAY 1945

May was a month of constant drenching rain, and the men of the 74th were always fighting the mud and dampness which interfered with everything they did and created a gigantic oppressive mess. On May 1st, Major General Archibald Arnold, Surgeon General of the U.S. Army 7th Division was admitted to the 74th Field Hospital as a patient. He was operated on for appendicitis. Lieutenant General Simon Bolivar Buckner Jr., who was in command of the entire 10th Army forces on Okinawa, visited General Arnold there.

To my Sweetheart:

Hello, my Darling! You were really sweet today by bringing me ten air mail letters. They made me so happy, Honey. You can't imagine how much better my morale is now. They were written 9, 10, 11, 12, 13, 14, 15, 16, 17 and 18th. Boy, I really spent an enjoyable evening reading all those letters from my sweet wife. Now I'm going to spend a couple of hours answering them. I also got a letter from my folks.

Today was another busy day as usual. I was so tired at seven that I decided to quit even if the work never gets done. Then I got five gallons of water and proceeded to take a bath. I even shaved for a change. I feel a little better. I'll be dirty again soon as I leave the tent. I also got a haircut today because it was so long. I couldn't even comb it any longer. I had it cut a little shorter than usual but didn't get a butch. You told me not to. After I got cleaned up I sat down to read my mail. I have just finished. It is ten o'clock. The mosquitoes are terrible tonite. I guess it is because it is raining outside. I suppose it will be muddy again tomorrow. The ground was getting dried up so we could get around.

Johnson is lying in his cot reading a book that he is interested in. I just told him he had better stop reading his book and write his Momma so she will be getting mail too. He received eleven letters today. Now he is one ahead of me. Maybe I'll get one tomorrow and be ahead of him.

You asked about Wally in your letter. He is getting along fine. We see each other every day, but we are so busy that we don't have time to talk much. He receives mail from Velma regularly, but he doesn't say much about her. I guess they are getting along a little better now.

You wanted to know if I had made out a will. No, I haven't as yet. I just never thought about it until I got here. Conditions won't permit us to at the present. I'm going to make out one soon as possible. I know I should have made out a will long before now, but I never thought about it. I guess I was too busy thinking and worrying about you. You are so sweet. I love you so much, why shouldn't I worry about you, Darling? Gee, Mommy, your sweet letters make me so lonesome for you. I never miss shedding tears when I read them. I love to cry over you, Darling. I realize what a sweet and precious wife you are to me.

I have to laugh when you tell me about you and the girls getting into arguments. I can just see you stomping your foot on the floor and telling them off. You little devil, you are just like your poppa. I love you for being that way too.

The early letters in May were not dated like the later letters in March. The war was hot and heavy with many casualties for both the United States and Japan. According to my research, the loss by the Japanese was fifteen per one American. In early May, Merle received ten letters from me because he was not allowed mail during the several battles taking place on Okinawa. The mail was held up during the Army and Marine hand-to-hand fighting with bayonets and mortar.

MERLE AND VALENTINA MARTIN

I received the letter and clipping telling about Dave's death and will send the clipping back to you. It surely took a long time for the war department to notify her. Gee that is really terrible. Valeria thought an awfully lot of him too. They made such a nice couple. This damn war surely has broken up a lot of happy homes. I hope it ends pretty soon because a year of this kind of life will make an old man out of me.

It kept raining and raining. Tropical temperatures were hot, and mosquitoes were on a rampage. Merle was busy and hardly had to time to read ten letters. Wally, Johnson, Gusler, and Merle did not have time to talk. Wally was receiving mail from Velma. Merle noticed this since he helped Johnson with the mail. Sending mail by air was finally bringing in four letters at a time.

Merle wrote on May 3rd that he only had three hours of sleep. By that date, the 74th Field Hospital could finally date their letters. Merle wanted letters from me so badly because he was so depressed. He also needed a shower. There wasn't any way for his unit to shower, and Merle was in the process of building one.

May 3, 1945
10:30 p.m.
Sweetheart:
Hello Darling! How is my sweet Mommy tonite? You were very sweet to me today by bringing me four air mail letters. They were written on April 19, 20, 21, and 22nd. Gee, Mommy, they made me so happy and raised my morale a lot.

Today has been another busy day as usual. I only got three hours of sleep last nite and then got up at 6:00 this morning so you can imagine how tired and crabby I am. Starting tonite I put one of my men on nite duty so maybe I'll get a little more rest. Then I'll have a little time to write to you.

We are now permitted to date the letters so you will know how old they are when you receive them. I am enclosing a little of the kind of money we are using now, a penny, nickel, and a dime. Boy when I do have a pay day, I'll need my barracks bag to carry it around in. This will be more for your scrapbook. See Honey I am always thinking of you. The chaplain got hold of some Mother's Day V-Mail greetings so I'm sending you one, your mother and my mother. I thought they were pretty nice.

So Betty Nelson is pregnant. I'll bet she is a mess to look at. I can't believe she has settled down but hope it is true. I'll bet Pa Nelson won't do so much boasting now, will he? She will probably have a "prize" for a husband when he comes home.

Betty Nelson was an old girlfriend of Merle's.

In this May 4th letter to me, Merle reported that he was now growing a mustache. After a later photo, I thought that he looked quite good with his black, curly whiskers that matched the hair on his head. He also wanted me to send him a black leather band for his watch, which he said would cost only a dollar.

The next day, a generator stopped working at 11:30 PM. Merle had my name painted on all the generators by a soldier in his unit who he said was a talented artist. I hope that I was not responsible for this. On May 3rd the 74th Field Hospital lost its first patient—their first death. The hospital was proud of the record it had made since admitting its first patient on April 26th, only nine days after they first set foot on the island. During that time, the hospital increased its capacity to 440 beds, which were filled quickly because the fighting was still heavy at the battle for Shuri Castle which consisted mostly of hand-to-hand combat with bayonets. The infantry was doing most of the fighting.

Honey one of my generators just stopped so I had better go and try to fix it. By the way, I had your name painted on all of them the other day one of my men is a very good painter so I had him decorate them up for me.

I hope I'll be able to find a little time tomorrow so I can write you a long letter. Anyway you know I am thinking about you and loving you with every ounce of my heart every minute of the day. Here's a big hug and lots of sweet kisses for you Darling. I'll see you in my dreams. Good-nite sweet dreams and

MERLE AND VALENTINA MARTIN

God Bless you and keep you safe and sweet for me only. I'll always be your true and faithful husband.

Under Germany, rumors of the end of the war in Europe reached the men fighting on Okinawa. Word spread quickly that Germany had finally surrendered. None of the men knew whether the news was accurate because they were accustomed to frequent rumors, most of which turned out to be false alarms.

May 8, 1945
Tues. nite 9:00
Sweetheart:
Well another day has gone by without any mail from you, Darling. I'm so lonesome for you that I don't know what to do. I hope you received a letter from me.

We received word today that Germany had officially surrendered. I don't know whether to believe it or not. We have heard so many false reports. Anyway I hope it is true because that will shorten the war over here. It shouldn't take so long to clean up the Japs and then poppa will be on his way home to Momma. Boy that will be the day won't it Darling?

It has been raining ever since yesterday and everything is a mess. I was mud from head to foot when I came in tonite. Johnson went to see if there was any mail and he also got soaked. What a life. Honey, you can be thankful that you are in the good old U.S.A. Tonite I helped Johnson make two mail boxes. We had a devil of a time with nothing much to work with but finally got it done. I have a piece of aluminum from a Jap plane that I am going to make a bracelet for you with as soon as I get some time. Several of the boys already made one and they look pretty nice.

Confirmed news of the surrender of Germany reached them on May 9th to the great relief of everyone. All the same, they continued to face a fierce and determined enemy—Japanese soldiers who had been trained to fight to death and very seldom surrendered. One Japanese commander ordered his men to trade each of their lives for ten U.S. soldiers or Marines. There was not much hullabaloo about Germany's surrender because the men in the Pacific were so busy fighting their own war. Then Merle didn't receive any mail from me for eleven days again which made it seem like years instead of months since we had been parted. I read about the heavy casualties on Okinawa and listened to news whenever I could after working at a job with lots of overtime.

Honey, about you getting a job working nites is all off. Now this is an order, I want you to obey it. "Do not work any place other than where you are". By that I mean you work days only. If you run short of money, write a check. Don't worry about the money we have plenty to get along on.

Merle and the unit worked on their foxholes because with all the rain, they were constantly full of water. Our hometown newspaper, "The Star Clipper," was not telling us about the troop movements. Merle was really downhearted but soon received five letters from me with the picture and folder and stationary I had sent months earlier. Merle's close friend Johnson took his responsibilities very seriously and enjoyed keeping the men happy with mail from home. Johnson would catch hell until the men got some mail, but once they did, he was restored to favor. Merle and Johnson were very busy making mailboxes for Johnson's mail room, and they kept at their work under very trying conditions.

Merle's good friend, Nathan Johnson, in Okinawa.

Dear Valentina

All this time food was poor. Their dinner was either stew or hash. Merle and Johnson used up their supply from Hawaii. From now on, they would have to make "moonlight requisitions." Johnson's wife later sent him a ham, and he and Merle had a feast.

Tonite Johnson and I were hungry so we dug down into our supply and got out a can of peanuts, a can of fruit cocktail, and a box of cookies. Now we will have a good lunch before going to bed. We brought quite a supply with us but it is slowly giving out. Things like that really taste good after eating this damn stew and hash. If I get over by the ration dump one of these days I'll really police me up some canned fruit. You know me and my moonlight requisitions. Ha! Remember how I used to eat two pieces of pie alamode at George's in Blackstone and then you would ring up a dime sale. I really get a laugh when I stop and think of all those free steaks you would give me when you worked there. They always say that anyone who can beat a Greek is pretty smart.

Letters from me were coming four to six at a time depending on space because supplies for the fighting men kept coming into Okinawa as well. Soldiers from the 96th Cavalry Reconnaissance Troop were assigned to guard the 74th. The homes of the men seemed so far away that by this time they had lost their personal concern. All of them longed for the end of the war.

On May 13th, Merle wrote that he and the boys were so tired of C-rations, and he was actually beginning to dream about the food at home, especially the steak and peach pie I would make for him on occasion.

Colonel Damron gave Merle two days' work to do for him and apparently told him that it did not look as though he was going to get the promotion that he was expecting. One of the generators stopped working, and it was Merle's job to fix it and keep it running. Once that task had been completed, he had to haul sand for the floor of the mail tent. For two days, he was busy creating an air-raid shelter during which he got only three hours' sleep while he was working on it. This heavy work is the reason behind my not getting a love letter on May 12th. Only a V-Mail came, which was a single small page big enough for only a brief note.

Merle also added a porch to the tent that he shared with Johnson so that they could stay dry, though nothing could keep the water from the foxhole that they shared and that they had to use frequently for refuge during air-raids. He remarked in his letters that citizens back home in the U.S. had no idea how terrible the fighting and suffering was for the troops. Photos of Gusler's new baby girl, now three months old, brought some happiness and a sense of connection to life at home to Merle and his close buddies.

The baby looks pretty nice. Gee, Darling, I wished we had a little baby girl just like you, don't you Honey? Then you wouldn't have to work. You could stay home and take care of her.

Today is also our wedding anniversary Darling. Just think I've been married to the sweetest girl in the world for forty-one months now. That fifteenth day of December was one of the two happiest days of my life, the other day was the day I met you. Darling I'll never forget those two days as long as I live. You are the sweetest girl in the world Darling, and the "only girl" for me. Please always stay sweet and true to poppa in every single way because I love you with all my heart, body, and soul.

Though we were actually married in December, Merle celebrated our anniversary on the fifteenth of every month while he was away.

To the great delight of the men of the 74th, a group of female nurses arrived in a C-47 transport plane on May 15th. At this point, air-raids had become less frequent, and when Japanese planes did come, they were seldom successful in their attempts to prevent drastic reduction in the number of trained pilots ready to fly missions for the Japanese forces. One reason for the decreasing number of air attacks was the drastic reduction in the number of trained pilots ready to fly missions for the Japanese forces. The kamikaze attacks that killed so many sailors and destroyed so many ships were in part a compensation for this lack of skilled Japanese fliers. Though extremely heavy gunfire from the many ships anchored just off shore and the numerous screening flights of fighter planes from the bases on Okinawa and the Navy carriers shot down most of the suicide planes before they could come close to their targets, many kamikazes did penetrate the protection and they did a tremendous amount of damage. About 5,000 sailors died as a direct result of these attacks, and multiple ships were sunk or badly damaged. For the Japanese, death in a suicide attack was considered glorious—it was an honor to die for the Emperor, according to the indoctrination given to soldiers and pilots by some Japanese military commanders. Kamikaze pilots were given enough fuel only to reach their targets—a one-way ticket to certain death.

Nurses of the 27th Station Hospital departed on May 16th. Merle reported on that day, his unit had admitted a patient who had been shot in the left side of his chest, where the human heart is situated in normal persons. This soldier, however, had developed his heart on the right side as a result of an illness. This anatomical abnormality, which made the news back home, saved the soldier's life.

Merle had to run the shower three times a day because of all the rain. No one else knew how to operate it because of its obsolete parts and unique construction—made by Merle. Again, Merle wrote of making more cases for the mail-room and doing it despite the endless rain and mud. The misery of the troops was intensified by the tropical heat and relentless mosquitoes.

May 18, 1945
Fri nite 10:30
To my Sweetheart!

MERLE AND VALENTINA MARTIN

Hello Darling! How are you tonite? I am very happy because you brought me six letters today. They were written on April 30, May 1, 4, 8, & 9th. I think that is pretty fast service, only 8 days for a letter to get here. I also received a letter from my folks and a V-Mail was returned to me that I wrote to Dave soon after we landed. It was marked March 7, and said unable to deliver to that address. I guess he is really gone, poor kid. I sure feel sorry for Valeria, and his folks. I can realize what a shock it was to them.

Today was a busy day as usual and I worked until 9:30 tonite, then Gusler came up to my tent and we talked about olden times. Guess it will be a long time before we will be able to have a good time again. It makes me so blue when I stop to think about all the good times we've had.

Honey, I surely was glad to receive the clipping about Howard Wilcox. I guess you never knew him very well but he is a swell fellow. He and I were real pals all the time I was in Waterloo and were always together until I met you. He never smoked or drank and was a clean boy. Boy what I wouldn't give to shake his hand.

Your letters made me very happy today Darling although I was sorry to hear that you got infection in your ear and hope it is alright by now.

Honey I wasn't peeved about you spending so much for your fur coat. I told you that I didn't care how much you spent on clothes or for yourself as long as you stayed true and faithful to me. That is what I'm interested in Darling. You know that is why I didn't want you to work at Rath's because I know what types of girls are there. I worry so much for fear they will lead you astray. So they wondered why you were staying true to me. What kind of girls are they anyhow? Darling you know what I think of people like that so you had better use your will power. You know what would happen if you did anything wrong, and I would find it out too because I know all the angles. I'm sure you wouldn't spoil our love affair just in order to have a little fun, would you Darling? Please don't be angry with me for talking this way but I love and worship you so much that I wouldn't have our love affair ruined for the world. I worry so much because I've seen so much of that stuff go on. I don't see why so many people let their a— run away with their brain. Mommy dear if the girls down at Rath's are that way quit your job. We can get along without the money.

I'm glad you got something for Mother on Mother's Day. You are such a sweet momma and you think of everything, don't you Honey?

By the way I have a watch that I've traded for. It is a fifteen jewel Bulova and is a pretty good watch only it needs a little fixing. I'm sending it home to you. I want you to have it fixed and give it to your Dad. He doesn't have a watch and I thought maybe he would like one.

Honey Dear I'm not going to answer all your letters tonite. I'm going to save some so I'll have something to write about tomorrow because I don't really expect any tomorrow.

Washing Machine Charlie was over a while ago so we had to spend a little time in our fox hole. It is eleven o'clock now so I'm going to kiss you good-nite and get in to bed to dream about my sweet Mommy. Darling my dreams are the same as yours. I would explain them in detail but I don't want the censors to get a laugh out of it. I always dream about you every nite regardless of how tired I am.

Here's a great big hug and lots of sweet kisses for the sweetest girl in the world who is none other than "You Sweetheart." I pray every nite before I go to sleep that your love for me will never die and that you will never be untrue to me in any way. You know if anything like that would happen Darling I'd just as soon die because you are what I am living for. Good-nite my Darling, God Bless you and keep you safe and faithful for your lonesome husband. Remember I love you with my heart, body, and soul and will always remain your faithful husband as long as you are true to me.

Forever & Ever

Merle

MERLE AND VALENTINA MARTIN

Howard Wilcox, a member of the infantry on Okinawa, had been shot in the arm, so he was out of commission for a few days. This allowed him to visit Merle several times and give him a break from his seemingly endless work.

On May 19th, the moon was so pretty and, Merle and I were so far apart that his letter was especially full of longing and romantic thoughts. Of course, I was just as lonely for him, though I was not in the state of constant, intense fear that the men lived with daily. I only missed him. Merle asked me to donate money for Catholic masses to be said for Dave. His weariness with the war—shared by all the troops—began to find expression more and more often in the letters from May.

I had sent Merle a clipping from the Courier newspaper that contained a story about his friend Howard Wilcox. That night, a single Japanese plane that had been sent nightly to harass the troops with bombs—called "Washing-Machine Charlie" because of the rhythmic pulsing of the plane's engine—forced Merle into his foxhole. Wilcox himself appeared on Okinawa on May 19th, and he and Merle had a good visit—a welcome reminder of life as it was back home. The rain continued to fall, and at one point, the tent ropes became so shrunken and taut that the lights ceased to work. Merle wrote that he had been working so hard that there was not even time for a craps game and of course, no pay-days.

On May 20th, Merle reported the hottest day he had experienced thus far. He had to fix generators after dark after receiving a call to fix them. The next day, it was still raining on Okinawa. Howard Wilcox came to visit again, and they shot at a four-foot snake that had gone under a wood pile. The men faced rain, rain, and more rain, but the water still had not come into the tent that Merle and Johnson shared. They had placed a native mat on their tent floor which they found earlier; the natives slept on two-inch mats like this one.

Wed. nite 8:30

DEAR VALENTINA

May 23, 1945
To my Darling wife:

Hello Honey ! How are you on this rainy nite? Are you as lonesome for me as I am for you? It has been raining all day again today, this makes three days of rain so you can imagine how muddy it is. We almost need a canoe to get around in. The roads are really slippery. Today when Johnson went for the mail a big truck hit their Jeep and scared the devil out of them.

During one of his souvenir collection hunts, Merle acquired a Filipino bill which Major General Arnold signed for him so that he could send home to me. I was racking up quite a collection of artifacts from Merle's time overseas.

Fri. morning
May 25:

Sweetheart:

I'm sorry I couldn't write to you last nite but Washing Machine Charlie came over and we had to spend the nite in our fox hole, so I am writing you this morning. Now you will get two letters today. I hope you will forgive me Darling. You will, won't you?

Today is another rainy day and the mud is belly deep again. I thought we would have a few nice days but guess this is our rainy season. Honey you didn't bring me any mail again. My morale is terribly low so please bring me a stack of it tonite. Johnson saw them unloading some yesterday so maybe it was for us.

In spite of the rain, Merle received the leather watch band that I had sent him. He said it fit perfectly. Colonel Damron's foxhole was full of water, so Merle helped him drain it. The rain was causing so much extra work. Merle said that he would rather be a private again and wanted me to take care of myself so that in 46 years we could celebrate our golden anniversary. The next day, his tent was still dry, but his foxhole had filled with water.

Later, a big truck knocked down his wires, and he was mad about it. It was, of course, still raining. The next day, electric wires were breaking down and had to be fixed. It even rained so hard that the tent wires snapped.

Colonel Damron took a picture of Merle who was dirty with mud and the rest of the problems working on a generator. He told me he would share the photograph. If he shared it, I never saw it. Shortly after, the Colonel also spent a week in bed with sinus problems. He told Merle that it was a sinus infection.

Merle began itching from fleas that he got from his floor mat, which he immediately threw away. The temperature on Okinawa at the end of May was so hot, so keeping himself clean was a task in itself. Merle was not the only one trying hard to maintain personal hygiene, but he was feeling the burden of the other men's dirtiness. Because he was in charge of the mechanics, Merle had to be at the showers so he could turn the water on for the men, and he also had to refill the water when they were empty—hard work just to keep the boys clean.

By now, Merle and I had already been apart for over six months, which seemed like forever.

Tues Nite 9:00
May 29, 1945
To my Darling!
    Honey dear you surprised me today and brought me a letter. It was written on May 20. I don't know where the ones in between the 16 & 20 are but I'll probably be getting them in a couple of days. Honey, what happened to your eye? You didn't say in your letter except that it was swollen and blood shot. I hope you didn't get popped by one of the girls. Surely you haven't been in a scrap. I hope it is better by now Honey because I wouldn't have you hurt in any way in the world.
    Well we had a day of sunshine for a change today. It really seemed good to see a little of this mud dry up. Tonite it is all cloudy again and showering some more so I suppose tomorrow will be another rainy day. We have a barracks bag full of dirty clothes and I don't know when we will get them

washed. If it doesn't quit raining pretty soon I'll have to visit Gusler and get some new ones.

I was really busy today. I went over every bit of the electric wiring and checked it to see if there were any bad wires. I'm so sore from crawling tents that I can hardly move.

Tonite I had my first bath in four days. I was beginning to smell so strong that I couldn't sleep with myself. Johnson and I heated about ten gallon of water so we both had a good bath. I also shaved and washed my hair so I'm all cleaned up now. How about making love to me now that I'm all cleaned up Mommy? You make love so nice. You sweet Mommy you. I sure would love you to pieces if I had you here. I'm so lonely for you, Darling that I've a notion to try to swim the Pacific only I'm not a very good swimmer.

I feel so sorry for Valeria. A person has to overlook some of her meanness at a time like this after having such a shock. I still think the best place for her is at home for different reasons. You know what people would say if she went somewhere else to live. I'm afraid you and her wouldn't get along so good if you had to live together and besides I don't want you living in a strange place. See Mommy dear, I'm giving out orders again, aren't I?

How much does my sweet momma love me tonite? As much as ever? I hope that is with every ounce of your heart because that is the way I love and worship you, my Darling! Always be a sweet and true Momma to me in every single way so we can always be the happiest couple in this wide world. You will, won't you Darling?

Honey dear, I've ran out of news again so will have to kiss you good-nite until tomorrow. See I've already written you more than you wrote me so if you would write more I could write you longer letters. I'm going to keep at you until you do. I'm an old meany aren't I Honey? I'm not to you though, I just want more of those long letters like you used to write me. I bet I'll get them won't I Honey?

Here's a great big squeeze and lots of sweet kisses for the sweetest wife in the whole world who is none other than "You

Darling." Good nite and sweet dreams, Sweetheart! I know I'll have sweet ones about you. God Bless you Honey and keep you safe and sweet for "Me Only." I'll always remain your faithful and loving husband as long as I live.

JUNE 1945

By June 1st, Gusler had new pictures of the baby girl named Mary Ann. He was really a proud poppa. Merle and Johnson, above their regular work of taking care of mail and making sure the 74th had electricity for all the tents and hospital including refrigeration, were busy. So much was going on with the infantry and hand-to-hand fighting, plus the hospital was operating around the clock with a growing list of patients. Merle and Johnson then were making a frame for their tent to prevent it from getting taut with so much rain so they would not lose their electricity and dry shelter. Merle claimed it was now better than the Colonel's and looked more like a house. Despite these improvements, it was still a rough life—mud to work in and "C" rations to eat. Merle was still worn out and said he had no appetite which was unusual since he always cleaned his plate. He felt something was wrong. I could tell by his letters when he wrote that he felt war was going to last a long time. It was surprising to me since I believed he wanted me to feel optimistic. Previously he had kept saying "This war can't last long," but that tone had now changed. He must have been very ill or very depressed. He kept writing that he was not able to stay caught up on his work.

Sun nite 8:30
June 3, 1945
To my Darling!

Hello Honey! How are you on this blue Sunday nite? Do you still love me? You were very sweet to me today and brought me a letter that you wrote me Sat. nite May 26. It was pretty short but very sweet and it made me real happy. What are you doing tonite? Writing me a really long letter, I hope.

Did you get rested up over the week-end? I suppose you heard all the gossip of the week. Why is Valeria quitting Yordy's? She maybe doesn't make such good wages there but I bet she makes more clear money than if she were working somewhere else and paying board and room.

Today was a rainy Sunday so I took life pretty easy. This morning I went to church and hauled a little sand to put around our tent so we wouldn't track mud in our tent. This afternoon I slept from one until five. I was so tired and still am from tromping around in the mud. It is raining hard out now so I guess tomorrow will be worse. What a dull life this is, "C" rations to eat, lots of mud, and above all you aren't here. If you were with me, I wouldn't mind putting up with all these hardships. I get so lonesome for you that I don't know what to do. I could sit right down and cry. I may be a sissy, but I surely love and worship my sweet Mommy.

How did your folks manage to get a "B" book? It must be a little easier to get gas now.

I'm glad you had your eyes tested and are getting new glasses, Honey. Only I wished you hadn't gotten those google eye frames. I never liked them. Just pay for your glasses with a check so you will have them out of the way and besides you already have too much coming out of your wages.

Howard W. remembered you and asked all about you. He said I did a very good job when I picked you for my wife and that you seemed to be a very sweet girl. I told him he didn't know the half of it, you were the sweetest wife on this side of Heaven.

According to Merle's rendition of the war, ten thousand American troops came back to the U.S. and arrived in New York from the European Theater of Operations because of Germany's surrender in early May. Merle and Johnson were still busy since the war in Japan was still on. In addition to building the wind- and rain-withstanding tent frame, they screened the front and back to make it cooler to sleep in and to keep mosquitoes out. It kept on raining, but they were hell-bent on keeping their tent dry. It was muddy around the tent so they hauled in sand to also keep the rain outside. There was so much mud in fact that the gas had to be carried in by the soldiers since trucks would get stuck in the mud. The hospital was also still a tent, including the surgical unit, so the rain and mud was just as much of a disturbance for it too. A Catholic mass was now held for the patients. Catholic members of other units and their own nurses and soldiers attended. These were being held regularly now.

I surely hope Marvin V. is safe. So he is in the infantry. Well, I know what he is going through wherever he is at because I see everything here. I don't think you need to be alarmed from not hearing from him for a while because he probably doesn't have time to write. This war is surely terrible and what I can't figure out is after they take an Island, they don't have a damn thing except some bare land and a few trees. Just think of the lives that have been sacrificed for these worthless places.

My cousin, Marvin V. was also drafted into the service in June 1945 and undoubtedly would be an infantry replacement for a fellow soldier. Merle knew from experience what a tough job that would be and kept Marvin in his thoughts.

I hear by the news that 10,000 troops landed in New York. Boy, I'll bet they are a bunch of happy boys. Probably Al Ploen will be coming home soon. Do you see Phylis very often? I wonder if they get along very good. I'll never forget how he treated her when she came to Virginia to see him. That was an awful way to act, wasn't it, Honey?

There were rumors about the war ending in six months. As yet, we were still at war on Okinawa and did not think it was possible according to Merle's letters. He thought he would probably be home in a year. Of course, at that time six months sounded like forever, so a year seemed nearly unbearable. I guess we were both blue.

Merle wearing a Japanese revolver.

DEAR VALENTINA

Wed Nite 10:30
June 6, 1945
My Darling!

How is my sweet momma tonite? Are you as lonesome as I am? I hope you are, Darling, as you will know how I feel. I didn't get any mail from you today. The roads were so muddy that we couldn't get to the post office, but we are going tomorrow. I am going to drive Johnson in the Weapons Carrier and we'll get there too. You know I never started any where yet that I didn't get there, have I, Mommy? Today was a real nice day. The sun was out bright and it dried up a little of the mud around our tent. We live on a hill so it dries up pretty quick.

I washed this morning after finding out we couldn't get to the post office, we both took the afternoon off. We cleaned our tent up, changed our bedding and really fixed it up, then we took a bath and put on clean clothes. It was about three-thirty by that time so we slept until supper time. The roads have been so bad that we couldn't get after any rations so we don't have much to eat but after supper Gusler came up with a case of fruit cocktail that he big-dealed someone out of so we had a good feed. We visited until nearly ten o'clock so that is why I got such a late start in writing to you.

One of the boys received word from home yesterday that his wife had died while giving birth to twins and they also died. That is really terrible and I bet it was an awful shock to him. He already has two children so that really makes it bad. I guess we both have a lot to be thankful for after all that we are well. That is the main thing because this war can't last always and if we both stay well, we are young yet and have a long life ahead of us. Isn't that right, Honey?

The bad roads and ten miles from the island post office made his life miserable. Now he wanted more packages from me. Roads continued to be muddy, making it difficult to get mail because not even Army trucks could move through the mud. True to his word, Merle successfully drove Johnson in the weapons carrier to get mail at the post office which was ten miles away. It was the only vehicle that made the journey

While I was at Fort Sill I met a working girl from Iowa. Her name was Ruby Bruggeman. In 1944, I got an announcement that she had a baby boy. At that time her boyfriend was in the service too. She married a Mervyl Olson who I had not met. We remained friends until her death. Her father worked at Fort Sill as a carpenter. Her parents had Merle and me out to his home then.

In one of my letters to Merle that month, I wrote about the second son in the Herman family being killed. He knew their parents. The Hermans had two boys and a girl. Wars are not selective about whose children they take.

I'm sorry about the other Herman boy being killed. That makes two deaths in their family now. This war sure is terrible, isn't it Honey? I guess you and I have a lot to be thankful for, don't we?

Mail was irregular because of the fighting, and equipment was needed for supplies for the fighting men. Merle was writing me every day, and I was writing him every day. Mail would not come in sometimes for several days at a time. It was the 8th of June when he was finally permitted to tell me that he was on Okinawa. He now had a new APO number: 902. He also received his battle star for the Battle of Okinawa. Now he was getting mail from me in ten days. He received a clipping I sent him from "The Star Clipper" about the circumstances of Dave's death on Iwo Jima. It made him feel awfully downhearted.

Hello my sweet Mommy! How are you tonite? I don't have to ask you how much you love me tonite, I know because you brought me three very sweet letters today telling me all about how much you love me. They were written May 18, June 1, & 2. I guess the one of May 18 was one that came part way by boat! I was sure glad to get it because I had a blank space in my letter file for that day. Now I am all caught up to date including

June 2. I also received a Vmail from Betty and the April 6 issue of the Star-Clipper. It was the one telling about Dave being killed on Iwo. He looked so nice in that picture. It was his wedding picture, wasn't it, Honey? This is sure a cruel world. They were such a happy couple. I really feel sorry for Valeria. No one realizes how bad this war is until it brings bad news to their own homes.

Merle was very concerned about his mother's health. He also could not remember her birthday. Other than that, he was very considerate and concerned about her. My mother told me that a man who is considerate of his mother would make a good and loving husband. I still believe her sixty-five years later, because it was true of the man I married.

On June 13th, Merle wrote that the hospital staff was operating on a wounded soldier's eyes. In the middle of the surgery, the lights in the hospital went out, and Merle was quickly summoned to repair them. It seemed that without Merle running the mechanical elements of the hospital, many necessities would have been lost.

One hot day in June, a rat as large as a cat (according to Merle) appeared near his and Johnson's tent. Merle acted quickly and chased it with a carbine, shot at it twice, and missed. They say war changes a man, and I believe that too because this was the same guy who was afraid of a little mouse that ran across the floor in our Macomb Apartment when we were at Camp Ellis.

Howard continued to stop by and visit Merle which helped them both keep their spirits up. Since his injury, Howard was taking it easier, so Merle saw him quite frequently. He told Merle that he remembered me. Up until that time we had met only once. Howard visited Merle several times throughout June. One day, he told Merle that his sweetheart was working at Blacks Department Store, and since nylon hose were rationed, if I went there and told her I was married to Merle, Howard's old friend, she would secretly sell me the nylon hose. Merle was now officially serving his country and sneaking me stockings. Toward the end of June, Howard was sent to Guam Hospital and later stateside for more treatment for the gunshot wound in his arm. At that time, Howard had already spent two years overseas and was now beginning to pay for it. We never saw him again until after the war, after he had married his sweetheart working at Blacks Department Store.

Colonel Damron was ill again with his sinus problems. Merle visited him, and they listened to a California station on the short wave radio. Later, when he saw the colonel again, he told Merle to take the radio and fix it. Apparently it was too noisy.

The men at the 74th were always hungry. They often went to the supply tent and got canned beef and fruit cocktail for dessert while a tough war was going on not too far away. Merle claimed to have eaten a quart of ice cream that day as well. Despite all the extra effort he put in to find better food, Merle did not gain any weight. This warranted a lot of teasing from his friends.

Two United States Infantry Army divisions and two Marines were fighting hand-to-hand with bayonets and motor shells against the Japanese soldiers. They too needed replacements like our Army and Marines.

Around the 12th of June, their amphitheater was in operation on a southern slope from the hospital. The movies were still interrupted of course during the most interesting part of the movie. When search lights began the air raid sirens went on. The movies would stop and the troops all watched the sky. After a short interlude which had become a regular occurrence, the all-clear sounded, and the movie was turned back on again. Sometimes there were several interruptions, so the movies had to be finished in installments. The men would bring Hershey bars from the Red Cross supply or something from the PX to munch on at the movies. The only thing that did not work quite right was the speaker system, but it was better than nothing. Of course on those nights, Merle worked at the PX. He did not like the lovemaking scenes in the movies because as he explained in his letters, they painfully reminded him of us.

DEAR VALENTINA

Today was another hot day and I almost burned up it was so hot. There isn't even a breeze tonite. They built an open-air theater because it was too hot inside a tent that no one would go to the show. They finished it today so I had to wire it all up. They had their first show tonite and it really worked nice. I stopped in for about ten minutes to see if it worked alright. There will be a show every nite now as long as we can get the film.

Musick got hold of some ham today through some big deal so they invited Johnson and myself down to supply for supper tonite. We had fried ham, corn, potatoes, cherry pie and coffee. Gusler did the cooking except for the pie. We really had a good supper and afterwards we visited for about an hour and then Johnson and I left. We were already to start writing letters when the air raid alarm sounded and it was so hot in our tent all shut up that we had to wait until it was over so we could leave the tent open.

Mommy, this hot weather is really getting me down. I don't know how much longer I can stand it. I've been so tired and weak the past few days and don't even have an appetite so you know there is something wrong.

By the middle of the month, the enemy was pushed from the southern part of the island to around Naha, the capital city. The fighting was fierce, but the men knew that the island would soon belong to them. The patients keep coming in and the hospital was kept full. The rain began to let up, and to their surprise, there were a few days without any rain. Two Red Cross workers also joined the outfit.

Sat. nite 10:00
June 16, 2945
To my Darling!
Honey, you really surprised me today by bringing me five letters. I also got one from my folks. They really made me happy except for one thing. Darling I feel so bad about you wanting to leave my folks and get an apartment with Valeria.

87

Merle and Valentina Martin

In Mother's letter, she also told me how bad they feel about it. Here I didn't know a thing about it until you wrote and said you had one rented. I know you feel sorry for Valeria and I do too, terribly sorry, but afterall she could get a room by herself because she would have to live alone sooner or later. You asked me what I would do if I were in your place and it was my brother, well I'd let him get a place by himself because in the long run, he would be just as well off. Darling, you know that there is <u>nothing</u> I wouldn't do for you but there are a few things that I am strict about.

When I left you promised you would live with my folks until I got back and I was so pleased. We are now permitted to make out allotments and I was going to make out a ten dollar allotment to mother to take care of your board so you would have that much more for yourself. My folks always treated you nice, didn't they Honey? Please stay at home for my sake, Darling. I beg you to. I'm sure you will, won't you, Honey? They were always so proud to have you and mother always told me about it in her letters. I may be a little old-fashioned in my ways and a little selfish but I love you so much, Darling and am so proud of you that I always want you to be my ideal. You will have to admit I am usually right in the long run.

It wasn't hard for me to imagine how upset Merle would be about me moving in with my sister. I already knew. I could tell he was worried about me moving in with her. The war continuing and his being homesick didn't help much either.

I read Ruby's letter that you enclosed. She surely is a swell girl and is one of the few that looks on married life the way they should. Her husband should really be proud of her. I bet they really worship their little baby and I'm terribly sorry now that we didn't have one. She would be so much company for you and then you wouldn't have to worry about working. She would keep your mind occupied and keep your home taking care of her. I'd love her so much.

DEAR VALENTINA

Merle's crisis about me moving from his folks' when I had promised I would stay was becoming increasingly upsetting to him. My parents wanted me to live with my young widowed sister who they felt should not live alone in the city. Merle did not go to church that Sunday possibly because he was still upset.

June was a trying month for everyone it seemed. The 74th Field Hospital was being rearranged and the Seabees (CBs) were building a Quonset hut for the surgical patients, and the lights had to be changed around. That was Merle's job, but he was still repairing tents from the rain. Weaver had been in the hospital for several days, and by now they had discovered it was pneumonia, made worse by the fact that he did not have the comforts of home to speed up his recovery. This left Wally running the motor pool by himself despite his bad leg. Merle helped Wally when he could, but the generators were also so weak that Merle had to make sure the others had lights in order to write their letters to their wives and sweethearts. Generators were stressed, and most had to be repaired usually done at ordnance. Merle was also a master carpenter so he built a supply tent for utilities so that he would have some storage. In addition, the weather was so hot that all the men were stripped down to almost nothing. Patience, strength, and appetites were all wearing thin. It seemed that the men could each write a book about all their war-related troubles in the month of June alone.

Merle was also shacked up with some mosquitoes in Okinawa, and it seemed that they bit him more than they bit an average individual. He had type A-B blood, which he believed was tastier, so the mosquitos always bit him first. Shortly, he and Johnson put the screen doors on his tent in order to keep the mosquitoes out.

By June 18th, Okinawa was secured. The Army and Marines were just mopping up. The enemy was defeated, captured, or pushed into the sea on the southern tip of Okinawa. A cliff on the southern end of the island was called "Suicide Cliff." Many Japanese soldiers leapt to their death there. Naha was captured even though much of the city was bombed by

United States Navy ships and destroyers. The fighting was limited to a small area south of Naha.

As the month of June continued, Merle kept telling me not to leave his folks because they wanted me as much as there as much as he did. Despite his plea, I decided to move into an apartment with my sister and two other girls. He was still upset and took it out on himself by writing that he was selfish for expecting me to stay with his parents. After he opened the PX, he forgot about my move for a while since mail was reaching him several days after it had been written. He enjoyed his work at the PX and got some experience in being a businessman, but Merle wrote that once the war was over, he was going to take it easy.

Thurs. Nite 9:30
June 21-45
Darling!

I received two sweet letters from you today which were written the 11, and 12. I sure was glad to hear from you, Honey, because I've really been down in the dumps lately. I see you have moved already. Honey, I thought you weren't going to move until you heard from me. It was a shock to me because I thought you were content staying with my folks. Anyway I hope you and Valeria get along alright. I suppose I'll never get any more long letters now because you will be too busy with your housekeeping and having company for supper, etc. Please don't be angry with me, Honey, for talking the way I do but I really feel bad about the situation. I guess I'm just old-fashioned but I love you so much, Darling, that I want you all for me and I wanted to always take care of you in my own selfish way. I know I'm just a no-good old selfish devil though, aren't I Honey?

Today was another hot day. It rained a little early this morning but didn't amount to much. I worked like the devil as usual. It seems like I have more work to do every day. I guess it won't hurt me any. It keeps my mind occupied. I'd go crazy if I wasn't busy all the time.

DEAR VALENTINA

I guess I told you we were opening up a P-X of our own. I'm going to work in it too because that will be a little extra money for me. I want to get every dollar I can get my hands on because I don't intend to do a damn bit of work for a while after the war.

Gusler received seven letters and some pictures from his wife today. His little baby girl is really growing. His wife always addresses one of her letters to Gus from their baby. He says she grew up in a hurry and writes him every day.

There began to be more leisure time for the troops. Then men of the 74th Field Hospital now had time for baseball, basketball, and volleyball. The lumber for the basketball court came from the Seabees and was located by the day room. There were many interesting games between officers and enlisted men of the organization. Softball teams were quite good and had a high standing in the Medical league of the island.

On June 20th the Commander of the Tenth Army, the highest ranking officer, was killed in the war. He died shortly after the battle for Shuri Castle which was taken by American forces. Prior to that, it was reported that he had been planning to visit the 74th Field Hospital. The men were so disappointed when he didn't appear. Now he never would because a piece of shrapnel had hit him, and he died immediately after the battle.

The island was declared secure on June 22, 1945. Earlier that day, a crippled Japanese plane started for the 74th Field Hospital. All the men were terrified that it would crash into the hospital. They held their breath as it came nearer and lower over the bay. At the last minute as the pilot approached the docks, he made a quick left bank and plunged into the side of an LST. There was a burst of flames followed by billowing smoke only a few hundred yards from the hospital. In a short while, the LST sunk at the dock. It was saved after several weeks were spent repairing it. Several Navy men were hurt and were brought to the 74th Field Hospital for burns and other injuries. At the same time, Weaver was finally on his way out of the hospital on June 26th, greatly welcomed by his friends who were more than glad to have him back. On the same day, Gusler and the colonel talked about returning to the "Golden Gate in '48," a phrase that began being passed among the boys, although they hoped they would be returning before then. When I received Merle's letter telling me this, my heart sank. To me, 1948 seemed like a lifetime away.

On June 27th, Merle and the boys had a real treat: real bread, fresh eggs (after months of the powdered kind), and fresh fruit. It was rumored that they would have steak for dinner. The rumors proved to be false, but it was veal, so they did not complain.

A Marine entertainment group also put on a show on the 74th basketball court. The Marine group had a hypnotist who had Howard "Dutch" Cronkleton do some weird things. Dutch was from Davenport, Iowa and helped Merle at the PX. Merle liked him. After the show, Dutch could not remember what all had taken place. He saw a photo of me later, and Merle invited him to come to his tent to show him a larger picture of me. He looked at it and said, "Boy, you can't beat the Iowa girls," and he eventually married one in Davenport with whom he created a lovely family of five children.

That night when Merle opened the PX, he was so hungry that he ate a whole package of cookies with no regrets.

Even though Okinawa was secure as of the 22nd, there was another bad air raid on the 29th. Merle and Johnson dove into their foxhole, without thinking twice about what they were wearing...or not.

I didn't even take time to put my pants on.

That night, a suicide plane dove into one of the 74th Field Hospital's supply ships.

By June 30th it was still unbearably hot, and Merle was still overhauling generators. He hoped that with a little more work, everything would be in working order again. On top of that, he was still working at the PX and taking inventory regularly. He was earning some money, but at a high cost. It was unbearably hot on the last day of the month with temperatures nearing 100 degrees Fahrenheit during the day.

I worked pretty hard today. I overhauled another generator. I only have three more left and then I'll have them all in good shape and ready to go again.

We finally finished taking inventory in the P-X. You see we have to take inventory twice a month. We are closed today so that will get me a little rest.

I'm just dead tired and it is so damn hot that we can't even get any rest at nite. Boy if I could just find a cool place somewhere I bet I'd sleep for a day. Our tent is like a bake oven all day long.

How much do you love me tonite Darling? Are you staying home and writing me a real long letter telling me all about our love affair and how sweet and true you will <u>always</u> be to me? I hope so Darling because that is what I want to hear and what makes those goose pimples come out on me. Oh Honey! I love you so <u>very</u>, <u>very</u> much. Maybe you will bring me two or three letters tomorrow so I can write you another real long letter. Tomorrow is Sunday so I'm not going to do any more than I have to. I'm going to church in the morning and pray for you Darling – that you will <u>always</u> be sweet and true to me in <u>every</u> single way and that God will bring us back together again <u>very</u> soon.

JULY 1945

By July 1, with Okinawa declared safe, the 74th appeared to have some down time—in most instances, making changes for the Occupation of Japan. Six nurses were released from the 74th Field Hospital and sent to the 27th Station Hospital.

For seven months now, I had been missing my handsome, kind, and caring husband. It was a long time ago when I said and kissed him goodbye at the PX at Camp Robinson, Arkansas. We were still 12,500 miles apart with the war continuing with Japan. Preparations were being made to occupy Japan which still might be years away. Merle was working at the PX, busy supplying the hospital and the 74th with electricity. They were busy as the war was planning to move forward in Japan.

A little break came on Sundays, while the boys attended Mass and listened to Sammy Kaye on the radio singing "An Hour Never Passes," one of Merle's favorite songs while he relaxed after lunch.

At the beginning of the month, Lieutenant Musick got a hold of a Japanese pistol which he had Merle put on over his shorts. He took Merle's picture and sent it to me once it was developed.

Wed. nite 9:30
July 4
My Darling Momma!
Honey, you were very sweet to me today and helped me to enjoy the 4th of July by bringing me three very sweet letters. I wished it was a year ago when we would be together making love. I'm so lonely for you, I could cry. I celebrated today by making me another house. They made me move to a different

area so Johnson and I had to build us another home. Boy, was I ever mad. We just got things fixed up so we could be fairly comfortable and now we have to move. This army life is killing me, Honey. Why don't you stop this damn war so I can get those civilian clothes on again to make love to you the good old-fashioned way.

There are lots of rumors of it being over this year but I don't believe any of them. Lets hope and pray that it is true anyway. I want to get home to you so bad so we can get a home of our own. You know, Darling, if this war wouldn't have come along, probably by now we would have had a nice home and also our baby girl that we both want so badly. If I could get home and have a home, our little girl, and most of all <u>You</u>, Darling, I wouldn't ask God for any thing more, I'd be perfectly satisfied.

So Valeria received all the particulars on Dave's place of burial etc. Honey I could have told you that some time ago if the censors would have allowed me to. I know more about him but guess I'll have to wait until I come home to tell you. What did they do with his personal items such as his watch, billfold, and ring? I suppose someone cabbaged on to them. Poor kid, I feel so sorry for him and Valeria also. This war has certainly broken up a lot of happy homes in many ways. Honey, don't say anything to Valeria about what I've told you. I can tell you one thing that I know all the particulars about him.

Well, Honey, I guess Wallie will be leaving us before long. His leg is really bad and I guess there is nothing that they can do for it so he will be sent back to some general hospital and possibly the States. I believe today was one of the hottest days we've ever had. I was just as wet as if I'd fell in the ocean all day. It hasn't cooled off much tonite either so I don't know if I'll get much rest or not. I hope so because I'm really tired.

What did you do today, Honey? Did you work hard at the office? Don't put in too many hours, Honey because I want you to have plenty of time to write me lots of long love letters every day. How much do you love poppa tonite? As much as I love you? You better, Darling, because I'm yours completely and forever. You are all I live for and without your love and your being an awfully sweet and true mommy, there would be no pleasure in my living. Don't ever forget that statement, Darling because it comes from the bottom of my heart. I don't think I'm exaggerating a bit when I say we are the happiest and most perfect matched couple in the world, don't you Honey? Let's be sure we always stay that way. I know I'll always do my part and I'm sure you will do your part too, won't you, Honey? If this damn war would only end so we could be together and have a home of our own. That is what I'm waiting for.

Well, Weaver just came from the show and stopped in to tell us that the Colonel made a farewell speech and that he is leaving to a different assignment. Things are really happening over here. By the time the war is over, we will have a brand new outfit.

I expected the enemy to pay us a visit today, but so far they have not been over to lay any eggs.

Those kinds of remarks made me feel uneasy. Communication was not much better which did little to ease Merle's worrying about his mother's health. It took 12-14 days to get an answer from home. Merle was also worrying about Valeria and thinking about her memorial service for Dave after his death on Iwo Jima. He admonished me in his letters not to tell Valeria what he knew about Dave's death but said that he would tell her himself once he got home. Merle had not even told me much about Dave's death. It was not something he shared lightly. He was still writing me every day about his love for me, and he wanted to be sure I was getting mail every day like he was.

It was looking like the Army was setting up for occupation soldiers. What troubled me was that it looked like it might be Merle's group. The soldiers were sending many packages home undoubtedly of souvenirs in case they had to be the Army of Occupation of Japan. If this happened, they would not be able to keep as many of their artifacts with them. Merle sent me the little teapot and dishes he found as well as some Japanese money for my scrapbook.

On July 7th Merle wrote that his sleep was interrupted by what he thought was a Japanese plane overhead. Comments like these did not sit well with me, though all that seemed to worry Merle was that he wasn't able to sleep through the night.

Talk of going home began to circulate through the air along with the hopeful possibility of the war being over within the year.

The 74th was getting fresh meat, so Merle had to set up a 5,000-pound refrigerator to keep the beer, meat, and pop cold. It even had a four cylinder motor.

Early in July, Colonel Damron was released from assignment. In his farewell address, he applauded the men and women of the 74th Field Hospital and said it was the best group he ever worked with. They had lost their activating officer and the man who had led them through the campaign. His "this is it, men" had become the byword of the men in the 74th. The men worked hard and all did their best when all the hospital beds were always full. Merle and his friends hated to see Colonel Damron go. Four days later, Lieutenant Colonel Harry M. Cowell was in charge.

With both Wally and Colonel Damron leaving, Merle was becoming more and more blue. He was really going to miss them both. Merle wrote that he worried about Wally's leg a lot. In the midst of these changes, he received two more letters from me and cried because they compounded his lonesomeness. He missed me as much as I missed him.

Eventually Merle was transferred to the Motor Pool as an ambulance driver and was happy with that job. He enjoyed all automobiles and knew quite a bit about them.

Honey I finally succeeded in getting a different job. I've been trying to get into the motor pool ever since we've been here. I never liked my job and besides, I've been doing three men's work. If I would have kept on with this work much longer, I would have ended up in the hospital as a nervous wreck.

Tomorrow morning I start driving an ambulance so maybe I can gain back a little of my weight and get to feeling a little better. I understand they are having two men to take my old job. They always expected too much from me so now they will maybe see what I've gone through. I think I can still hold my rank but don't care anyway because I wouldn't ruin my health for a measly $16 a month. You don't blame me, do you, Honey? I don't want to ruin my health in any way because I want to be able to smooch you when I'm eighty just as I did the day we were married. Money doesn't mean everything in this world. To me, happiness means everything. Don't you think so, Darling?

Today I didn't do much except work on my ambulance a little. When I get it all cleaned up, I'm going to have a sign painted on the radiator, "The Bohemia Special". Don't you think that is pretty cute? I'll send you some pictures of it. I think I'll put another sign on the back, "Martin's Meat Wagon". Ha! Anyway, I can have a little rest once in a while now because all I will do is take care of my vehicle and above all, I will take care of poppa for his Darling momma!

During July, the men were being sent to other hospitals, and Merle was writing passionate letters to me. He felt that since the war was over, he would be heading back to the United States soon. I went along with his feelings since I too wanted him home now that the war was over. His letters were very heartfelt and lonely for me since he had more time to think about me and about coming home. His letters became more passionate and driven, and they made me believe that he would be on his way soon. I was anxious to have him come home and have our life together again, but July only brought more of the same torment about our future, and the pain of waiting to go home would last many months more. Merle wrote that he would still be smooching me when he was 80 which turned out to be true.

Dear Valentina

Valeria got a job as a lifeguard at the public swimming pool in Waterloo. I knew that this was going to create a crisis between Merle and me since my parents did not want her to live alone. She was eighteen and widowed. What could I do?

Merle also asked me to send him a pair of sandals, something he could wear on his feet that weren't as hot or cumbersome as his work boots.

When we lived in Little Rock, Merle found decks of cards in the landlord's closet. Now he was selling them to the soldiers after payday for some easy money. As a result, more poker games were popping up around the camp.

Also in July, Merle went with Weaver to visit his cousin's grave. He, Johnson, Gusler, and Weaver had more time now for reflection and reminiscing about their lives before the war.

Friday Nite 7:00
July 20
My Darling Momma!

NO letter today so I'm very unhappy tonite. I'm writing you while working in the PX because there isn't much business tonite. We are all sold out of every thing except cigarettes. Tomorrow we draw new supplies so I suppose we will do big business for a few nites.

It rained all day today so things are pretty muddy. I had the PX all cleaned up and now you should see it. I got wet last nite too. It was so cool and I was really sawing logs when it started to rain so by the time I woke up my bed was damp. I was half asleep when I did get up to let the sides of the tent down and I got soaked doing that. I had a nice midnite bath. Boy, if anyone ever mentions camping out to me after the war I'll whip them.

We didn't get a paper today so don't know what the news is. I hope the Japs are ready to give up. You know Honey I was just thinking today how it will seem when the war is over and we are sitting around waiting for a boat to go home. Boy when I get to San Francisco they better have my discharge waiting for me because I'm not waiting for it. I'll grab me a handful of freight cars and be on my way home to momma in no time flat. All the M.P.'s in Frisco couldn't hold me. Won't that be the day Mommy? We will start on another honeymoon as soon as I get home so we can be all alone. We will really catch up on our loving, won't we Honey?

I didn't do much today. I didn't even go out on a trip. This morning I worked on my ambulance a little and this afternoon I helped Weaver. I'm getting pretty well caught up on my sleep so now feel a little better.

Did you have a busy day at the office today? Honey, don't work too hard. I want you to have plenty of time to write me lots of long letters every day telling me how much you love me and how sweet and true you will always be to me. By the way how much do you love poppa tonite? As much as I love you? Darling, I hope so because I love you with every ounce of my heart, body, and soul and am yours completely forever as long as you stay a true and faithful Mommy in every way, and I'll take care of the rest. You will never be sorry, Darling, I promise you. Please excuse this stationery I am using. I have better, but this is all that was here so guess you won't mind. Did you see the folks today? I hope they are both feeling good by now.

Well, Honey, I've got to close the PX now and clean it up for tomorrow so I'm going to kiss you good-nite and get to work. Please bring me lots of mail tomorrow so I can write you a real long letter on Sat. nite.

Here's a big hug and lots of sweet kisses for you to go to sleep on. Good-nite Sweetheart! Sweet Dreams and I pray that God will always keep you safe, sweet and true always for me only. With every ounce of my love for you Darling, I'll always remain your loving, faithful, and kind husband –
Forever & Ever
Daddy.
Good nite mommy!
Always be sweet to poppa.

Dear Valentina

Sat. Nite 10:00
July 21
My Darling Momma!

I just finished cleaning the P-X after a busy nite so will get started making love to you. Honey. We sold $216. worth of merchandise so guess we did pretty good. We drew a pretty good bunch of supplies today – candy, cookies, peanuts, and hair oil and shampoo, also fountain pens and quite a few other things. I bought me a Watermans pen for $1.75, and a cheap pencil to carry with me all the time and save the set you gave me. Now I'm going to shine them up and save them to use when I get home. If I lose this pen I won't hate it so bad. It works pretty good for $1.75, don't you think so Honey? I'm writing this letter with it.

I was pretty busy for a change today, this morning I made a trip to the other end of the Island and this afternoon I arranged all the supplies in the PX. I did take time to shave and shower before supper.

Tomorrow Johnson and I are going sightseeing. He and I are going for the mail in my ambulance and then keep on going and tour the Island and see the sights. I have it all arranged with Weaver, he is motor Sergeant now since Wallie is gone. We are going to take the camera along and take some pictures so I probably won't get back until evening. I surely like being in the motor pool again. That is the kind of work I like and besides I don't have to work near as hard. Wally is in Saipan now, but don't know for how long.

Today was really a hot day after the rain, the sun came out really bright and nearly burnt us up.

Honey, you brought me two very sweet letters today. They made me so happy but terrible lonely for you. Gee Mommy I love you so much. Why don't they stop this damn war so I can come home to you. I read a piece in the paper today where they expect the war to end this year and that raised my morale a little. It has to end this year because I can't stay away from you much longer.

Merle and Valentina Martin

Did you get a letter from me today Darling? I hope you did so you can write me a real long one tonite. What are you doing tonite Darling? I hope you are at home writing me and telling me how much you love me and how sweet and true you will always be to your lonesome poppa. You are aren't you Darling? By the way how much do you love me tonite, Honey? With all you heart and soul like I love you? Please do always Darling, I promise you will never be sorry. You know there is nothing in my power I wouldn't do for you, don't you? Just stay sweet and true to me in every way, and we will always have the happiest home in the world. To me that means everything, how about you, Honey?

In your letter you asked if I could spare five so I am enclosing a ten dollar money order for you. I'm glad you are getting the folks a nice anniversary present. You think of every thing, don't you Honey? You are such a sweet Mommy! I'll send you another ten dollars soon as we get paid so you can buy something for yourself. I'm getting a pretty good nest egg started so when I come home I can surprise you.

I'll be glad to get the shoes because these old G.I. shoes are so heavy. I put on my civilian shoes lots of evenings to rest these old feet of mine. They didn't cost much so don't care if I ruin them.

Honey, don't worry about getting so big that I can't paddle you when you are mean. That day will never come so go ahead and eat. You don't want to lose any more weight because 105 is not a bit too heavy.

Honey, I'm glad to hear you didn't go to the carnival because I wouldn't have liked it if you did. Please don't ever go places until I get home. There will be plenty of places to go then. Promise, Darling?

Well Honey dear it is getting late so guess I'd better kiss you good-nite and get into dreamland. I've got to get up early in the morning. I know I'm going to have sweet dreams about you tonite after receiving those two sweet letters today.

Let's hope and pray this war ends soon so we don't have to spend many more of these lonely Sat. nites apart.

Tell all the folks Hello for me and not to not worry about me, just take the best of care of my sweet mommy for me until I get home.

Bring me lots of mail again tomorrow so I can write you another long letter tomorrow.

Here's a big squeeze and lots of sweet kisses for the sweetest girl in the world, "You Darling."

Good-nite Sweetheart! Sweet dreams, and I pray that God will always keep you safe and sweet for "me only". With every ounce of my love for "You Darling," I'll always remain your loving, faithful and kind husband –
Forever & Ever
Daddy
Good-nite Mommy!
I'm warning you that you are really going to get the devil smooched out of you in my dreams tonite! Always be sweet to poppa!

On July 29th, Merle got caught in the rain on his way to do inventory at the PX, not an unusual occurrence at Okinawa. It would have made for a disappointing evening if Gusler hadn't showed up with some steaks that he had big-dealed from the Navy.

On the 31st of July, the men had another air raid. Not surprisingly, it rained, and they had to pick up fresh rations on the beach. Merle received another loving letter from me which helped him keep going through all the muck.

July rolled on warm and lazily as Merle and I dreamed about our life together on opposite sides of the world. I missed him and loved him with my whole heart, and it didn't take much for me to imagine that he felt the same way. It had been eight months since I had last seen Merle, and I was trying my hardest to be patient for his safe return.

AUGUST 1945

Wed nite 8:30
Aug 1 '45
My Darling Momma!
You made me very happy today when you brought me two really sweet letters. My morale was getting pretty low after not getting a letter for three days. I worry so much when I don't hear from you every day, Darling! I also received two rolls of film today which you mailed on July 21. Isn't that good service. Now I can take some more pictures to send home to you. Do you like lots of pictures of me, Honey? It's about time I was getting some more from you because I haven't had any for quite a while now.

It has been raining off and on all day and the roads are slippery as glass. I made a couple trips and was all over the road. It is still raining tonite and the wind is blowing to beat the devil. They predict a typhoon for tonite. Gee, I hope it gets sidetracked somewhere because if one would ever hit here, it would probably blow all the tents over. They are just like cyclones back home.

Several typhoons had come and gone, and more were expected. Merle and the rest of the crew had their fingers crossed tightly, hoping that the hospital would be spared. It if a typhoon hit, tents would go down, and there would be even more work to do.

From my letter, Merle learned that my sister received $300 from the War Department for Dave. Merle assumed it was Dave's pay. Valeria planned to put up a monument for Dave at the cemetery where his grandparents are buried and undoubtedly his parents would one day rest. My sister later received a picture of Dave's grave at the Iwo Jima Cemetery.

That is the way all the graves are fixed, Honey. They are covered with sand and a white cross at the head of the grave with the name on it.

In Okinawa, it was still raining, and the whole place was muddy. Rainy days and no daily letters from me made Merle very blue. It was nice that he and Johnson were close. He said Johnson helped him keep his sanity. It was so wet that the planes could not land at Yontan and Kadena Airports, and it was so muddy that Johnson didn't want to go to the post office either, so Merle put chains on his ambulance and drove him there. Johnson wouldn't ride with anyone else when the roads were bad.

Activity had lessened for the 74th Field Hospital since Okinawa had been declared secure on June 22. On Mondays and Tuesdays, Merle went to Naha for PX supplies. Their unit was having fresh food three times a week and was getting ice cream every other day made from dehydrated ingredients. All they had to do was add milk and water.

Mail was coming so irregular then. The rain must have been causing it. At least, that's what Merle suspected.

When Merle went to get rations, he took and ate 10 oranges which had not been available to them previously. He and the Mess Sergeant fried a steak and had a good supper. Fresh food came from the ships every two days and was taken off the hospital driver's truck.

I was beginning to wonder by now if I was just a memory to Merle. I knew that if this had happened, at least they would be fond memories as Merle often wrote that he loved me more and more each day since the day we were married.

MERLE AND VALENTINA MARTIN

Tues Nite 9:30
Aug 7
My Darling Momma!

Honey, you brought me two of the sweetest letters today. They made me so happy. I got the 27 yesterday and today the 25 and 26 so now I'm all caught up. I should get two or three new ones tomorrow. Gee Darling I'm so lonesome for you tonite, why don't you fly over and spend a few days with me so we can get caught up on our loving? You sweet Mommy. Darling you never need to worry about me losing any love for you. You should know better than that any way. I'll always love you with all my heart as long as I live and will do every thing in my power in order to make you a happy home.

I had to laugh about you losing the Hawaiian dollar bill even though it did make you mad. You screw ball and then you have the nerve to tell me to be sure and send it back. I told Johnson about you losing it and he laughed and said I should send you five of them so if you lost one you would have plenty more. I'll inscribe it for you and enclose it in this letter.

I sure am tired tonite. This morning I took Gusler to get some supplies and this afternoon I went for the PX supplies. I didn't get back in time for supper so had to bum a sandwich. I am really going to sleep tonite and maybe a little tomorrow if I'm not too busy.

As yet we haven't gotten any Parker pens, but expect some soon and when we do I'll send you one. We get plenty of candy and things like that. They told me we would be getting cokes in a few days and I'll be glad too because I really like them. It rained this morning and then the sun came out so it was another hot and sultry day.

I also received a letter from Betty today. She didn't have much to say that was new.

I heard over the news today that we have a new type of bomb that they are using over Japan now and that it is really powerful.

DEAR VALENTINA

An ultimatum was sent to Japan warning her if she did not currently surrender, she would have to suffer the consequences. Japan ignored the ultimatum.

In the history of the 74th on the 9th of August 1945, a fiery explosion "too tremendous to believe" transformed the city of Nagasaki into a dessert, killing many civilians. The tragedy shattered the foundation of Japan's security. So tremendous was the destructive force of the new weapon, the atomic bomb, that Japan already recognized her fate if she dared carry the war any further.

On August 9th, Russia declared war on Japan. Now with the atomic bomb, and Russia on the same side as the United States, it seemed that the war would be ending soon. Johnson woke Merle up to tell him the news. Merle told him, "I always believed that Japan would surrender six months after Germany." Eager to go home, the boys began betting on when the war would end.

While Merle's unit was at the movie tent, they were surprised to see the sky filled with flares and tracers. Officially the war was not over, but they believed it had been over in a matter of hours. Most of them were at the theater when it started. The movie was never finished. Everyone was shouting, whistling, and firing rifles into the night. It was the same all over the island. The Rock seemed to vibrate with excitement, revelry, and happiness. Thousands of guns and firearms of all sorts were fired. Everyone went slightly mad that night—shouting, whistling, and firing their rifles, according to Merle's letters.

Thurs. nite
Aug. 9
My Darling!
Well Honey a lot has happened since last nite, Russia has declared war on Japan. That is surely good news now with the new atomic bomb we have and Russia helping too. I believe the war will be over before long. That's the best news I've heard since Germany surrendered. Johnson woke me up at six this morning to tell me the news. He always gets up early.

MERLE AND VALENTINA MARTIN

I have been saying all along that Japan would surrender by or before November, six months after Germany and I don't think I'll miss it far.

Gee Mommy, I sure hope it is over soon so I can come home to you. They can't keep us apart much longer. You need me back home and I need you and I hope God knows it. Japan might give up pretty soon. The boys are doing a lot of betting already.

You brought me two very sweet letters today, Honey. They made me happy only terrible lonesome for you. You are such a sweet Mommy and I love you so much.

Darling, I'm so worried about your eyes. You take good care of them regardless of what it costs. I wouldn't have your eyes ruined for anything or all the money in the world. You did the right thing by quitting your job. I know it was an awful strain on your eyes doing that small figuring and you can find a lot nicer place to work even if it doesn't pay as much. Maybe you could get a job at Black's, you would like that kind of work and it wouldn't be hard on your eyes. Don't worry about the money Darling, just take good care of your health. That is the main thing. I'll send you some money as often as I can.

Honey have you decided where you are going to move yet. If Valeria wants to go home then you can move in with the folks and you won't have any expenses. I'll allot Mother enough out of my pay for your board and room.

I'll be so glad when we get a home of our own, then we won't have to depend on anyone, will we Honey?

Tomorrow nite the boys in the motor pool and supply are having an ice cream feed. We big-dealed the mix so we will have fifteen gallons. I bet I go to bed with a full belly tomorrow nite. Ha!

Yes Honey I know about the Japs blowing up a ship loaded with beer. The dirty devils. I would rather have cokes than beer though. We should be getting some before long now.

The day before, they went to the motor pool with the boys to eat up fifteen gallons of ice cream, and the same night the

Japanese blew up one of their ships which had beer on it. Merle had been to Naha getting supplies that day. The next day, he was starting a letter to me when the celebration began. The gunshots and shouting were so loud that Merle couldn't concentrate on his letter.

Honey I was just going to start a letter to you last nite when a big celebration started. I believe every guy in the outfit shot up all the ammunition we had and things were so noisy that I couldn't write. The report came over the radio that Japan would accept the Potsdam ultimatum. It hasn't been confirmed yet but I'm sure it will be today. Johnson and I sat up most all nite to see if we could hear any more news. Honey it was the grandest feeling, I'm sure peace is in the making now. Johnson and I kept talking about how glad we would be to be free men again and wondering how long they would keep us here. We might make it home for Christmas yet.

Gee Honey I'm so excited and happy I don't know what to do. I suppose you know more about the particulars than we do. Boy if it is over they better not keep me here too long or I'll really blow my top. I've been in this Army long enough.

The next morning, they found out the celebration was slightly premature.

Merle told me not to worry anymore since he would be safe and secure. He would be busy packing supplies and equipment, and of course...eating. Gusler came with more pears, and all the boys enjoyed them. Merle wrote that he was also packing an ashtray he made which Johnson would send after he left. It would be something to remember Okinawa in the future. He said, "Someday you can tell our children Daddy made it out of parts form a Japanese airplane."

Meanwhile, Japan and the rest of the world knew that the end of the war was in sight. The world united and watched to see what Japan would do. On the 14th of August, after much discussion and dissention, Japan gave the cease fire to all its forces while peace was being negotiated.

Thurs. nite
Aug. 16
My Darling Momma!

Well Honey, the war is really over. Isn't it a grand feeling? We heard the final news over the radio last nite on our way to this god-forsaken Island. Now I wonder how long they will keep me over here. Boy it hadn't better be very long or I will really raise hell. We spent the nite unloading our equipment off the boat.

I suppose they really had a celebration back in the States. Gee I wished I could have been there so we could have celebrated too. I don't see how they could keep us away from our wives and families too long, do you Honey? The war is over now so they should let us married men come home and the single men finish up the work over here.

This little Island is named Kume Shima and it is five miles long and three miles wide. They have a cemetery with only two graves on it. I'll get a picture of it to send you. It is about fifty miles from Okinawa. It is a hell of a place, no roads or anything and it rains all the time. Things are really rough here and I hope like hell we aren't over here more than a month. There isn't even a post office here. The mail is supposed to go out every day but I don't know when we will get mail, probably two or three times a week.

C Section of the 74th Field Hospital was on its way to Kume Shima. It was a great day for everybody even though there was not as much excitement and celebrating as there was for the "false alarm" occasion. Everyone felt good, and there were broad smiles and good cheer everywhere. Six officers went to Kume Shima. The C Section was to set up the 100-bed field hospital there for future use. Major Bacile was the Commanding Officer of the C Section. Major Leo D. Hahn from the 89th Field Hospital became the commanding officer of the 74th Field Hospital on Okinawa.

It took ten hours to deliver the C Section to Kume Shima. Merle wrote that they did their own packing and loading for the trip to set up the station hospital for the troops already located there. The boys worked long hours with no sleep until the hospital was set up. After that, there was not much to do. The hospital did not have many patients. What they had primarily was medical patients and not any surgical patients. There had not been any fighting on Kume Shima previously. At that time, Japan had not agreed to the peace agreement.

The C Section drove across the island in a Government Issued (G.I.) truck to another outfit to see a movie: "The Falcon's Brother" starring Tom Conway and George Saunders. Many of them went to the movies every night, and many had seen the movies previously in the States.

I was pretty busy today getting things fixed up but in two or three days I probably won't have much to do. A person doesn't feel much like working when there is nothing except C rations to eat. Boy when I get home, I want steak and pie three times a day. How about it, Honey? You won't mind cooking for poppa, will you? You are such a sweet mommy and I love you so much, they have just got to send me home to you right away. If they don't, we will write to the President, won't we Darling?

All the news I've heard so far was that they expected to let 5,000,000 men out by next summer. I still have hopes of being home around the first of the year or before. A lot can happen in four months. I think once they get started, they will get us home pretty fast. Boy will we build us a little home and have the best of everything, won't we Darling? You know I've been so nervous and my mind is in a daze all the time since the war has ended. I just keep planning and thinking all the time about us living together again soon. Since I've thought over all the narrow escapes I've had, I consider myself very lucky to be alive and in one piece. That is worth an awful lot to both of us, isn't it Honey? Even if we have had to be far apart for a few months, we can be thankful that both of us are in good health. We will make up for all the lost time when we get back together, won't we Honey?

Seventeen of the nurses left on temporary duty with their three Red Cross workers to the 23rd General Hospital. To pass time, most of the C Section spent its time following individual interests. Merle was searching for seashells that he could use to make a necklace and bracelets for me. Others played cards or volleyball, or went swimming. They used to play other teams rather hard competitive volleyball and baseball games in the area. They had some good volleyball games. The court was set up between the pharmacy and the mess tent and was the scene of some calm, coordinated teamwork until at times the "Greek," George Mariakas, would go on a rampage. A while after they had been there, an amphibious unit moved in just a short distance from them. The amtracs and water buffalo vehicles were used to bring in supplies from the LCT or LCIs that came in since they had no dock on the island.

Baseball was also popular in Okinawa. They had many games with part of the 24th Infantry Division which was made up of African American personnel. Those men were really good and though they always beat the men of the 74th Field Hospital, everyone had a lot of fun. Unlike Okinawa, the native living conditions on Kume were practically unimpaired by the destruction of the war even though the people were extremely poor in material possessions. They lived compactly in several small villages over the island. These villages were unlike anything the men had yet seen because they were not in shambles. On occasion, they were able to ride about and see the natives around their homes or in the fields, not in military settlements as on Okinawa but living more or less normal lives in a normal environment.

Meanwhile, back on Okinawa, the "mainland" hospital had received orders for another move, so the unit was closed and torn down to affect the move. Again, it was a big job, but it didn't take very long. On August 20th, the move was made, and a skeleton crew was left behind to police up where the unit had been on the beach. Merle flew in to get supplies for Kume Shima unexpectedly and surprised Gusler and Johnson.

Dear Valentina

Kay Kyser would be there the next day and Merle wanted to see his show. It was the first live entertainment on Okinawa. Kay Kyser and Isch Kabibble put on a good show accompanied by a United States band from the Philippines and USO girls. The boys had lots of laughs and liked the looks of the civilian clothes.

The signing of the peace agreement was delayed two days because of another typhoon had been predicted. It was to be September 2nd on the *U.S.S. Missouri* in Tokyo Bay.

While on Kume Shima, C Section watched the planes taking off for Japan to be there for the Army of Occupation in Tokyo. There was quite a bit of activity when they arrived at the new location, and by the 23rd of the month, they were able to receive the first patient in the new area of the 74th Field Hospital on Motobu peninsula. Motobu was about sixty miles north of the old area and on the opposite side of the island.

Merle was as passionate in his letters to me as they continued to arrive from Kume Shima. Many times he played more poker and my letters became shorter. I understand how he felt. I too felt the same way about him. By August 15th, he had been gone nine months which seemed like forever, and mail became irregular, so we often didn't hear from each other for days. I too missed his letters as much as he missed mine.

Tues. Nite 8:30
Aug. 28
My Darling Momma!

Hello, Honey! How is my sweet momma tonite? Are you as lonesome for me as I am for you? I didn't get any mail again today and it will probably be two or three more days before I get any. I don't know what I'm going to do. Well, Mommy, I finally succeeded in getting a plane back to the Island. I left at ten and was here in thirty minutes. It is fun to ride in those little cub planes. The pilot did a few tricks and thought he could fool me but he didn't scare me a bit.

So far the Yanks haven't had any trouble going into Japan. Gee, I sure hope those damn Japs behave so they will let us come home pretty soon. I can hardly wait until they announce what system they are going to use and how fast they will get us back home. There is quite a debate about when we signed up for the duration and six months. This morning I heard over the news that they are drafting 50,000 monthly between the ages of 18 and 25. I think that is a good idea, don't you Honey? Any thing that will get me home to my sweet momma.

They better get me home pretty soon, hadn't they Honey? Gusler says he will be home by Xmas so I shouldn't be far behind him.

How is everything back home? I suppose things are getting more plentiful every day in the stores. I heard over the radio tonite that automobiles will be about the same price as they were in 1942. I guess a new Buick would cost about $1700.

How much do you love your lonesome poppa tonite, Honey? As much as I love you? Gee I sure hope so momma because I'm so proud of you and love you so very much, if only I could be home with you, I would be the happiest daddy in the world.

SEPTEMBER 1945

On September 2, 1945, the peace treaty was officially signed on the battleship *U.S.S. Missouri* in Tokyo Bay. There would be no more fighting and no more false alarms. On Kume Shima, the men listened to President Truman and General MacArthur on the news. They had all wondered how much longer it would be until they would be able to go home. The war was over, but they had to be patient. That night, a typhoon hit Kume Shima where Section C of the 74th Field Hospital was stationed. Not much damage was done. A few days before the typhoon, several hundred barrels of oil were unloaded on the beach. The day after that, sea was full of barrels of oil. The rough waves brought in a lot of the barrels; the amphibian corps brought in the rest.

Well, Honey, today is the day the world has been waiting for three years and a half. The world is at peace again. Now if only I could be home with you. I wonder how long it will be. Today over the news they said everyone with 80 or more points would be home by November. At that rate I'll never get home because I only have 50. I don't think it is a bit fair to give 12 points for every child because we have men that have only been in the Army a year and with two or three children have more points than a fellow who has been in three years.

They are also letting all men over 35 years old out so there will be a lot of our men coming home pretty soon. That is going to really make me lonesome and all the more blue too. Gee Honey I don't see why I can't come home to you pretty soon. Surely they will lower the point score or do something pretty soon.

Darling, you won't mind waiting for me, will you? I'm sure you won't. It may not be too long. I still say I'll be home in six months and when I do we will make up for all the happy moments we lost out on, won't we? I'm going to save every cent I can get hold of so when I get back we can really take life easy and have the best of everything.

That day, Merle received twenty-one letters from me and others at home. Due to a lighting problem, the guys could not answer their letters because they had no lights after 8:00 PM. The C Section was waiting for transportation to Okinawa. Planes were not coming in because of the bad weather, and Merle had not heard from me since August 12th. He was downhearted.

Mon. nite 8:30
Sept. 3
My Darling!
Hello Honey! How does it seem to live in a peaceful world again? It would be perfect if only we were together, wouldn't it? I don't believe it will be so long. They said over the news today that we would get home as soon as transportation would permit so I feel a little better now. I'm sure I'll be home in six months or sooner. Gee, won't that be nice Honey? Then we can really make love and get our home that we have been wanting for nearly four years. Over the news today they said censorship would be lifted immediately so soon as it is I'll write you a real letter. I can say what I want to then and every one else won't know about it. No one needs to know about our love affair, do they Honey?
Well, Johnson will be getting out of the Army now because he is 35 years old. The best of his life has passed. Just think Honey, it will be quite a few years before we get that old. Sometime I'd like to go to North Carolina to visit he and his wife. We have been good pals ever since we left the States.
Honey write and tell me what your plans for our new home are. I am anxious to know and I think we both have the same ideas. Honey, I can hardly wait. I can just see the time

already when I'll be coming home from work and you will be standing on the porch waiting to greet me with a big kiss. You sweet mommy you!

Merle had been held up on Okinawa, so he hauled water and spent the rest of the day playing rummy and reading his mail. He couldn't stand to play cards for very long, however, because he and I had often played rummy while we were waiting to be transferred to another Army camp in the United States. The simple card game when played abroad was now making him lonely for me. It seemed like he was running out of things to do that didn't somehow remind him of home. Still on the 6th, his letter was censored. It was really butchered. He was afraid he might be sent to Japan to be in the Army of Occupation.

At this time, replacements were coming including new lieutenants from Officer Candidate School which the enlisted men called "90-day wonders." They were commissioned after 90 days of training once they were enlisted. Merle didn't appreciate that these new officers were censoring his mail.

Fri. nite 8:00
Sept. 7
My Darling momma!

Hello, Honey! How is my sweet momma tonite? Do you love me an awfully lot? Starting today our letters won't be censored anymore so I can write what ever I please. I sure am glad too because I didn't like the idea of these 90-day wonders reading my mail.

Honey, a terrible thing happened here today. Some Marines were fishing and blasting the fish out with hand grenades and a grenade went off in one of the Marines hands and killed him instantly. I had to go pick him up in my ambulance and was he ever an awful sight. He was torn with holes. It surely is too bad he had to lose his life after the war is all over. Just carelessness is all that caused it, but people don't stop to think. He was 24 years old and married so that means sad news to another wife. I've seen more terrible sights since I've been over here and I don't want to see any more.

Now I can tell you what I know about Dave. I talked to a fellow at the airport and he let me go with him on his mail run to Iwo Jima one day last May. I went over to visit his grave and to get a picture of it for Valeria. I got there O.K. and had only one hour to get to his grave and back to the airport so I hurried there. I took three pictures of his grave and two of the cemetery and when I got back to the airport, some Colonel saw my camera and took it away from me because cameras aren't allowed around an airport if you don't have a license. I knew it and tried to hide it but the damn thing was too big. This Colonel took my name and was going to have me court martialed but Damron got me out of it and got my camera back for me. This other Colonel had already thrown away the film. Boy was I ever mad. I tried to explain what I was doing with it but he wouldn't listen to me. When I get back to Okinawa, I'm going to try to get another ride over there if this pilot is still here. I rode in a C-47 plane and it was really a nice trip. Dave's grave was fixed very neatly. It was covered with sand and has his name, rank and unit on the cross. The Marine Cemetery is much nicer than and Army cemetery. The guard told me that a wooden casket was built for all of them. He didn't know Dave but told me some fellows names that did. If I would have had more time, I would have looked these fellows up. Gee was it ever a large cemetery. It is surely too bad we have to have war. Iwo Jima is a very poor Island and sure isn't worth one-third of the lives that were lost there. I hate it that I couldn't get away with the pictures but I did the best I could. I'm going to try to get back.

Well today was the day you planned to have memorial services for Dave. I sure wished I could have been there. I feel so sorry for Valeria and she is so young to have such bad luck. I think I could have had a lot of souveniers but I didn't go looking for them. I wasn't going to take any chances on running into a booby trap or mine. I wanted to be sure that I got home to you all in one piece. We had enough narrow escapes as it was. I'm not going to tell you about them until I get home.

DEAR VALENTINA

The unit listened intently to news broadcasts at the mess hall radio. The bill for men over 35 or with 85 points was in Congress. President Truman had asked Congress to continue the draft. That would allow Merle to come home earlier. He believed it wouldn't be too long because if it passed, he would no longer be a member of the Army of Occupation.

Merle, along with the rest of C Section, was anxious to leave Kume Shima. As always, he was constantly hungry because he had to rely on C rations to survive. Good and fresh food was difficult to find on the undeveloped island. The Kume Shima natives were leading normal lives, and the men were able to enjoy having them nearby. The war had not gotten to them. Their desire to leave was strengthened by the idea that they would be getting their mail regularly and having something to eat besides C rations.

Today was the official surrendering of this Island. There was a ceremony and all the remaining Jap soldiers gave up and turned in their arms. They will be sent to a P.W. camp tomorrow.

Hot weather and mosquitoes seemed to be a persistent annoyance for Merle and the other men. It was windy too. They got plenty of sand in their eyes because of it.

Today has really been a hot day. None of us wear any clothes here except a pair of G.I. shorts. This is a regular nudist colony. Ha!

On the 8th of September, General McArthur returned to Japan and raised the American flag on the American Embassy. By this time, two of the 74th Field Hospital men from C Section had left for home in the United States. Mobilization was over, but it would be some time before most of the men would be able to go home.

Merle and Valentina Martin

The typhoon on the 16th brought a terrible wind storm on Kume Shima, lasting 36 hours. When it hit, the un-tented had moved to the ward tent for barracks. The outfit had been warned that the storm was on its way, so the men who had tents made certain all the tent pegs were in the ground. Merle didn't write on the 16th. The typhoon blew all the tents down, and he wrote that things were a mess. Their equipment was all packed except for the tents. Those had not been taken down yet. Four of the drivers were dry because they stayed in a native house available nearby

We had a typhoon here last nite and it really wrecked the place. It blew all our tents down and was things ever a mess. We had all our equipment packed but hadn't taken the tents down yet. A typhoon is just about like a tornado except that it rains too. Us four drivers were pretty lucky because we were living in an old native house and it stayed nice and dry. This was sure a hell of a looking mess when we got up this morning. The boys have rolled all the tents up and gathered all the equipment up now so it looks pretty good again. The major and I got into a big argument last nite. He wanted me to go out in the storm and stake down the tents but I told him I wouldn't risk my life because the war was over and if he wanted it done to do it himself. I told him I wanted to go home one of these days. Boy was he mad. He said he had a notion to break me and I told him to go ahead that I thought my life was worth more than $16 a month. I was mad enough to fight. He hasn't spoken to me today so don't know what he has on his mind and I don't care. I've a good notion to report him to Tenth Army. These officers sure like to make slaves out of the men but they won't pull much on me.

Four vehicles were brought up from the motor pool and placed as anchors on each of the four corner of the large tent. It seemed like nothing would be left on the face of the island. The vehicles were the only things that saved the large tent. The next day, everyone came out to a scene of destruction. Tents were down in shapeless forms in the area. The personnel tent was left standing as well as a few of the officers' two-man tents. The tents were never put back up. Most of the men had already been alerted and were waiting to go back to the Motobu Peninsula on Okinawa. They had very few patients in the hospital. Sometimes they didn't have any.

We are still waiting for a boat to take us back to Okinawa but one hasn't come after us yet. I'm anxious to get back so I can get my mail every day.

Finally a boat came. It was raining, and the men rocked and rolled in the rain. Despite the ponchos they were wearing, the men were soaked. It rained for two days. By then, they were back on Okinawa, bedraggled and tired. The 74th truck picked them up and took them to a mess hall. They were happy when they found a bunk to rest in. After the men ate and had their spirits revived, a great bag of mail was brought to them. Most of the mail had been stopped for a week pending their return to Okinawa. A few days later, another typhoon swept through Okinawa.

Boy my morale is really high tonite. We heard over the radio that by Nov. 1 the points would drop to 60 and by Jan. every man with more than two years service would be discharged immediately. Now I know I'll be home by Jan. at the latest. Won't that be nice, Mommy? We will really make love then, won't we? I'll be so glad, then we can get our home and live a peaceful life.

Joining the Army was not so popular since the war had ended. However, Merle though everyone should try it to know what it was like to live a rough life like he had been.

The C Section nurses came in with the rest of group, and the day room had been completed a few days before the storm struck. It was built sturdily with lumber and had a corrugated tin roof. It proved to be the safest place in the hospital. When the strips loosened during the night, several men would brave the elements to nail them back into place. Many of the Navy's smallest boats were swept ashore by violent waves.

After the typhoon, it was decided that the unit should have only a 100-bed hospital. Using what was left, they would operate a much smaller facility.

Johnson and Merle were back together in their special tent moved from the beach on Motobu peninsula. It was still raining of course, but it was good to be back with the boys again. The night he got back, Merle talked with Johnson for a long time about going back home and how their lives would change very drastically. Merle took some pictures of the Japanese envoys and sent them to me when they were on Ie Shima signing the peace agreement. All this time, Weaver was sick in the hospital again.

Honey I said I wasn't going to play any more poker until next pay day but I felt lucky yesterday so decided to play a little. I was lucky too and won another $25 so guess it was worth my time. Now I am $90 ahead since pay day so I've done pretty good. I guess the reason for the boys playing so much poker is that they couldn't send any home because there isn't any facilities for money orders. I'll send you a nice little present when I get back to Okinawa. We signed the payroll yesterday for Sept. so in another ten days I'll draw $27.50.

I'm going to work in the PX when I get back too so that will be a few more dollars. The extra money will help out a lot when I get home, won't it Honey?

You wondered if we belonged to the tenth army – yes we were assigned to it in Hawaii. I tried to tell you in my letters but didn't know if you took the hint or not

Merle did not belong to the Tenth Army now. His clash with the new commanding officer of the 74th Field Hospital continued, and he continued to wait to be sent home with dwindling amounts of patience.

I guess I'll go back to work in the P-X starting Oct 1, so that will be $25 a month more money to have when I get home.

DEAR VALENTINA

Honey I plan to have quite a little money in my pocket when I hit Frisco. See Honey I am planning all the time for our new home too.

I received my battle star for Okinawa today so am sending it to you. It is to be put on that Asiatic-Pacific ribbon that I sent you from Hawaii. When I got it today I looked at it and thought to myself "that is small pay for keeping a man away from his wife".

I wrote the folks a letter today so now I'm pretty well caught up. I do owe your folks a letter yet, and I'll try and write them tomorrow.

Honey are you writing me a really long letter tonite telling me how much you love me and how sweet you will always be to me? I hope so Darling because your sweet letters are all that keep me going from day to day. It can't be much longer now until we will be back together again making love so let's just be patient and look forward to that day.

In my letter to Merle, I wrote that my parents would spend winter in California with my sister, Valeria, who had lost her husband. Merle was hoping that I wouldn't be joining them so that I would be ready to meet him at whatever station he arrived at when he returned home, and chances were that it wouldn't be in California. He wrote that he would be home within six months. I too expected him sooner, but now he wrote it might be before Christmas. Soldiers now with 80 points would be home in November according to radio reports. What a nice feeling it was thinking he would be leaving even if we could not be together, censorship would soon be over.

Today has been another hot day. It rains nearly every day up here on the peninsula so you can imagine how muddy it is.

Ie Shima is only two miles from where we are and we can look on the island from here. Johnson and I plan to take a trip to Ie Shima this Sunday and take a picture of Ernie Pyle's grave. They say Ie Shima is a pretty nice Island. So your folks are still going to California. I didn't think they would go. It would be a good trip for Valeria. Honey I hope you don't go because when I come home I want you there. I'll have you meet me wherever I get discharged and that will probably be in Illinois. I probably won't even stop in California.

There is a rumor going around that our outfit will be broken up in about sixty days and I sure hope it is true. If it is I'll get home around January. That isn't far away. Gusler has over 70 points so he will be leaving next month and Johnson will be leaving next month so all my buddies will be gone. Oh well, it won't be long for me either so guess I can wait.

They wanted me to take Johnson's place when he goes home but I didn't. I would rather be a driver and besides I don't want any important job. I'm almost sure I'll be home in January because our outfit will break up in December and then I'll be eligible to come home. Of course it is not for sure that it will break up then but our C.O. says in about 60 days.

The 74th Field Hospital had created a good name for itself because of their service to the patients and the number of lives they had saved. However, Since Colonel Damron left, the outfit was starting to go downhill. Many patients were being sent to large hospitals or home to the United States.

Lieutenant Musick received a letter from Colonel Damron. He was a psyche patient at Walter Reed Hospital in Washington, D.C. We suspected that was why Merle never got the promotion he was expecting during the early spring and summer when the battle was going on. Merle wrote that he thought Colonal Damron's anxieties were because of his wife who Merle heard was not being entirely faithful.

Oh yes! Lt Musick got a letter from Colonel Damron and he is in Walter Reed Gen. Hospital in Wash. He is a patient. They sent him back as a syco patient, in other words he went nuts. I think he worried himself sick about his wife from what I hear she was running around a little. Wallie is back in the

States and walking on crutches. I guess I told you he was operated on in Siapan.

Wally arrived in the United States before Merle, crutches and all, but he went through a lot of pain to get home early.

Toward the end of September, Merle worked late at the PX, taking inventory because they drew a lot of supplies a few days earlier. Inventory came out alright, but it made him late to write his letters to me. After that, Gusler also got a hold of some steak, and he, Johnson, and Merle had steak before they went to bed. They hadn't had fresh meat in a long time.

Merle's letters were full of nostalgia about being at home in the United States. He wrote that he was going to buy a zoot suit and a red tie and the he would be so happy driving with me down the street in our new car. As silly as they seemed at the time, Merle's daydreams turned out to be an effective survival strategy, preventing him from falling into a dismal state of mind because he was so far away from home and in such miserable circumstances.

Johnson and Gusler were leaving the next month to go home. Merle expected to leave at the same time with Weaver since they had served the same amount of time in the Army. To pass the time, Merle worked as a dispatcher for five ambulances, but they were not getting much use since there was no more 74th Field Hospital.

Honey what are you doing tonite? Are you terribly lonesome for me like I am you? I hope you are writing me a real long letter tonite telling me all about our love affair and your plans for a home when I get back. How much do you love me tonite, mommy? With all your heart like I love you? I hope so Honey because without __all__ your love there would be no pleasure in my living. You are all I live for Darling so don't ever let me down. Always be an awfully sweet and true mommy to me and you will be the happiest mommy in the world. I promise you Darling I'll do everything in my power to make you a perfect home. We will always have the best of everything.

Merle and Valentina Martin

Here's your big hug and lots of real sweet kisses for the sweetest mommy a fellow ever had. I hope and pray that we won't have to spend many more Sat. nites apart. God Bless You Honey and keep you safe and sweet for <u>me</u> <u>only</u>.

With all my love for <u>you only</u> Honey, I'll always be your loving, faithful and proud poppa------
Forever & Ever
Merle

OCTOBER 1945

By October 1945, the 74th Field Hospital was nearing the end of an era. Life was slowing down, and the hospital was usually not very busy. Merle was regularly checking the trucks at the Motor Pool and worked the PX. Most of the officers had already left excepting the motor pool unit and its supplies unit. The boys had a lot of free time too, so they continued to play volleyball, baseball, and went fishing in the China Sea behind the 74th refrigeration plant. The fish were brought home and cooked by private dinners in individual tents. Of course, it continued to rain.

Merle was so sick of Army life. All he and I both wanted was to be together again. He continued to express his intense desire to see me in his letters, but now he was equally passionate about getting on the boat to come home to Iowa. I was not afraid to admit that I felt the same way. I wanted him home too.

Replacements were coming in for those who were leaving. The rest of the men were told the 74th would be deactivated in November. The typhoon on September 16th had destroyed most of the tents which had not been reset. The men had been waiting to be sent to a place with new scenery either to Japan or to join another outfit on the island but were nostalgic about leaving their buddies in the 74th Field Hospital.

On October 1st, Merle was horribly upset because he learned that I was going to go to California with Valeria. My parents wanted me to go with her even though they thought about going there themselves, but having Betty still as a senior in high school, they did not want to leave her at home alone. My mother and father insisted I go with Valeria who already had a job as a telephone operator in Berkley, California. She felt that she could find a job for me, and the two girls—Mary Jane and

Ardys—from Rath's office if they came along. I knew that Merle would be unhappy if I went, and my parents would be unhappy if I didn't. Nobody was going to win.

Tues nite
Oct 2
Darling!
I received three letters from you today and one from my folks. Your letters were written 18, 19, and 21. Honey your letters brought sad news to me. You didn't tell me you were going to California and have an apartment with Mary Jane. Honey why didn't you tell me sooner? It really hurts me when you don't tell me everything. I tell you everything, Darling. I didn't like it so well when you had an apartment in Waterloo but I didn't say very much. I can't figure out why you have to go to California to live when I will be coming home pretty soon. Mommy I guess I'm just a mean and ugly poppa but I guess I'll have to tell you how I feel anyway. I won't stand for you living out in California with those girls. It is alright for Valeria to go but you are a married woman and you should stay at home. Honey I can't figure out why you wanted to go away now because it won't be long before I'll be coming home. I was planning so big how you would be at the train to meet me when I came home, and now when I get home you won't be there! I hope you won't be too angry with me for talking the way I do but Darling, I am so terribly down-hearted and hurt. I guess I don't know nothing about what is going on anymore. I have been saving every cent that I could get my hands on so we could take a nice vacation when I got back. Gee Darling I wished you would have waited at home for me until I got back. I know I'm mean and selfish but I can't help it, I love and worship you so terribly much that I just can't help it. Honey Valeria doesn't need you with her, why don't you go back home and make me happy?

Merle was obviously not pleased, and it soon developed into a crisis between the two of us. I wanted to go. My sister wanted me to go. My parents wanted me to go, and the two friends, Mary Jane and Ardys wanted me to go. Whether or not it was the wrong decision seemed to put me between a rock and a hard place. It was difficult to change Merle's mind, especially when he would soon be coming home, and I wouldn't be there to meet him. I could tell he was upset when I read his letters, and it was hard to convince him that it had nothing to do with our love for each other. It was difficult for both of us.

Honey I couldn't sleep last nite. I was awake all nite thinking and worrying about you. Honey why didn't you tell me you were going to have an apartment in Calif? Tell me truthfully. The only way you can prove to me that you love me with all your heart is to pack your suitcase and take the first train home. I hate to give you hell mommy but you have been a naughty girl. Surely your mother wouldn't want you living in an apartment with some other girls. I think I'll write to her today.

I didn't do much again today except lay around. I felt so rotten when I got up this morning, I didn't sleep a wink last nite. This morning I went on sick call to see what was wrong with me. The doctor said my nerves were what was making me sick. He gave me some pills to take every three hours and I have to go back every day. He asked me if there was something that was worrying so I had to lie a little and told him no. He told me not to work but to read a book or something to pass the time. I don't like to read though so guess I'll have to find something to do. Don't worry about me now because I'll be okay in a few days again.

Well Honey I suppose you are enjoying Calif. life by now. Are you thinking about me? Do you still love me with all your heart? Gee Darling I'm so blue I could sit right down and cry like a baby. I'm so lonely for you and then to have you go away makes it all the worse. I hope that by the time you receive this letter you are home again. When you get back home my mind will be at ease and not until then. Darling I can't stand to have you away from home. Please make your lonesome daddy happy and do as I ask you to--go back home and wait patiently for me. You will, won't you Honey? There will still be plenty of time for us to run around when I get home

Merle became sad, sick, nervous, and eventually developed hives because he was worrying so much. He pined almost the entire month about me moving with Valeria and seemed to forget all about the good news of him being able to come back to the United States soon.

Today has been a terrible day out. I don't believe I ever saw it rain so hard and the wind blew the rain right into the tent. We tried to keep it from raining in but couldn't and Johnson and I both got soaked. My bed is all wet so guess I won't sleep very comfortably tonite. We have some pretty bad storms here once in a while. It is real cool out tonite so guess fall is here. I guess we will be getting our winter clothes pretty soon. I understand from what the natives say that they get snow here in the winter.

I spent most of the day in the tent and didn't even go to supper again because it was raining so hard but I wasn't hungry anyway. I have been sick since yesterday and so nervous I couldn't even sleep. Honey what did you do with your dog? Did you ever get that watch fixed for your dad?

I didn't write to your folks about you going to Calif. I thought no use say anything to them about it. I didn't say anything to my folks about it either. I know my dad hated to see you go because he likes to have you around. Honey he thinks the world of you and would do anything for you that he would do for me.

Honey I know you will be mad when you receive the letter I wrote to you last nite. I don't want to be mean to you in the slightest way, but Darling it hurt me so terribly much. That no place for you to be out there where all those boys are coming back from overseas. If you would have only waited until I got home, then we could have gone together.

Dear Valentina

I got a laugh when I read Garabedian's letter. I'll bet he is really happy to be going home. I don't blame him a bit. I'll bet he will really celebrate for a while. Next summer I would like to take a trip and visit Johnson, Gusler and also Garabedian. Don't you think that would be a nice vacation? One of the doctors in our outfit, Major Roberts, has a movie camera and when he gets back to the States he will have a complete show of the 74ᵗʰ in operation. It shows me up on the tents putting up lights and everything. He said if I would come to his home in Panama City, Fla we could see the picture. I think it would be worth our time, don't you Honey? He and I are good friends. He said he would show us a real time if we would visit him.

Well Honey I guess I've told you all the news for tonite so will give you a big kiss and get in to bed. I hope you are being an awful sweet and true mommy to me and that you will be on your way home soon. Honey you won't have much longer to wait now and we will make up for all lost time when I get back. Please don't be angry with me and remember I love you with all of my heart.

Merle was still depressed and complaining about not getting home. The most recent typhoon had ruined Johnson's and his tent, making matters even worse. The storm happened on a Monday. On Thursday, he was still upset and wasn't able to write me for days. He had closed the tent as tight as possible, but despite his efforts, the rain still managed to find a way inside. Johnson and Merle held on for as long as they could but couldn't keep their clothes, beds, or anything dry. After midnight, they went to the motor pool, got into Merle's ambulance, took off their wet clothes, wrapped up in blankets, and turned on the ambulance heat to get warm. The next morning, the place was a mess.

Well Honey, a lot has happened since Monday. I suppose you have already heard about the storm we had, but I'll tell you how it ruined our home anyway. The wind began to blow about 5:00 in the evening and by 7:00 the tents were beginning to come down. Johnson and I closed our tent up tight and got inside of it. We tried to hold the front from inside but after a couple hours our arms were so tired we couldn't hold on any longer and besides it rained in and we were both soaking wet. Every bit of clothing we had was wet and we expected our house to blow over any minute so we laid down on the floor so if it did we wouldn't get hit by any boards. About twelve we were so wet and cold that we couldn't stand it any longer, so we went down to the motor pool, got in my ambulance and took all our clothes off and wrapped up in a blanket. I started the ambulance and turned on the heater so we could get warmed up a little. When we got up yesterday morning this was really a tough looking place. We had about 200 patients so yesterday we evacuated all but 60 of them. I drove nearly 300 miles yesterday and didn't get done until 9 last nite. When I got back I didn't have any place to sleep because my bed was still soaked so last nite I slept in my ambulance again. Johnson and I spent all day drying clothes and our bedding so we will at least have a dry place to sleep tonite.

Merle wrote that it was the worst storm he had ever witnessed in his life. It would take a month to put the place in order again. The typhoon even blew down their post office. Many of the men were hurt in the storm, and they had no lights. His letters to me were written by the lights in the ambulance. My letters to him had by then been lost in the China Sea.

To make things even worse, the roof was blown off the PX, so their supplies were wet. Cigarettes were stolen too. Merle had to do an inventory of the supplies and of course ended up short. In addition to all these troubles, there was a food shortage, because the food had been lost or spoiled in the typhoon.

Last nite after Johnson and I got in bed Gusler came over with some eggs so we fried them and had egg sandwiches and coffee. They really tasted good because our food has been very poor lately. I suppose you have heard about the food shortage over the radio. I heard over the news yesterday that Gen.

DEAR VALENTINA

Stillwell is going to evacuate all troops except a permanent garrison off the Island as soon as possible so don't suppose we will be here much longer. I sure hope they send all of us home. Gusler and Johnson expect to leave any day now. I should be home before too long myself.

On the 15th, the men were informed that all of the hospital patients were to leave on hospital ships. A very few of them would be well in two weeks, so about 50 patients would be leaving. It was a 52-mile trip to haul them to the deck.

I didn't do much today except clean my ambulance up a little and this afternoon I had my usual nap. If we just had some decent food to eat maybe I could gain a little weight. I have to get up in the morning at 4:30 because we are evacuating all patients that are going to be hospitalized more than two weeks to hospital ships. I suppose they will be taken to Siapan or some place like that. I guess they don't want many patients around because they expect some more typhoons soon. We have about 50 patients going so that will mean a busy day for me.

Finally a ray of sunshine appeared on the 18th for Merle.

Well Honey it looks as if I'll be eligible to come home in January. I heard over the news today that they expect to lower the points again in Dec. They will probably lower them to 50 and I only have 49. If they lower them to 50 in Dec, I'll surely be eligible in January. If they would count them up again in Dec. I would have 55 but I understand that the points won't be counted again. I should be home by the last of January. That means we will be apart three months longer and that is a long time but all we can do is be patient and look forward to the day we do get back together again.

The plan was to have only one station hospital on the island built like they were built in the States, and the service men would live in Quonset Huts. Things seemed to be moving along, and the boys could begin to see the light at the end of the tunnel. This, however, did not deter Merle's anxieties about me living in California. As October continued, Merle got more hives from the C rations and worrying about me.

Sat. nite
Oct 20

Well Honey I see you and Valeria have an apartment. I was hoping so much that you wouldn't. Of course it is alright for Valeria to get one if she likes it out there but I do hope you will do as I asked you to and go home. I may be old-fashioned but Honey I'd be so much happier if you would go back home and wait there. You don't have to work if you don't want to, just take life easy and wait patiently for me. That is the main thing. Honey I love you so terribly much that I don't know what to do. I'm sure you won't blame me for being so strict, will you?

So you like to work in the telephone office. Doesn't it get tiresome sitting so many hours every day?

I know Calif. is a pretty place and I would like to go out there myself sometime. Maybe in a few years we can afford a trip together. I wouldn't care to live there though, would you Honey? I wouldn't like that fog they have there so much of the time.

I haven't heard any more about our outfit breaking up only know it is scheduled to around Dec. 1.

Sat. nite
Oct 27
My Darling!

No letter from you today so this is a blue Sat. nite for me. Honey I wonder how many more Sat. nites we will have to be apart. I sure hope it won't be many more. I'm so lonesome for you that I'm almost crazy. How much does my sweet momma love me tonite? I hope it is with all your heart because that is the way I will always love you. Honey I hope you aren't angry with me anymore, I'm so worried because I wouldn't have you angry with me for the world. I always want you to be happy and content.

Today we all had to take influenza shots and they really make you sick. Tonite I feel just like I had the flu. I ache all over and have chills. It affects some people worse than others. I hope I feel better tomorrow. Johnson and I plan to go to Ie Shima tomorrow because it will be about the last chance we will have. He has a friend from his home town over there that he wants to see before he goes home.

I expect Johnson and Gusler will be going home any day now. Orders came in today for some of the high point men to leave tomorrow. The lucky devils, why couldn't I be one of them.

Officers were being transferred out either for discharge or relocation. Things were happening to bring the boys home, but for Merle and me, they weren't happening fast enough.

I'm so happy to know you aren't mad at me anymore. I was worried for fear that you might be. Honey I couldn't stand having you angry with me because I love you so darn much. It made me feel so good to have you say that you know I loved you with all my heart. I know you love me too Honey and I have absolute faith in you too. I love to have you tell me all about our love affair and how sweet and true you will always be to me even if I have to get you mad to tell me. Ha! Honey you are such a sweet mommy and I am so proud of you. I can <u>hardly</u> wait until we get our own home so we can do as we please. We will have everything then, won't we Mommy?

Today has been a busy day for me and I am pretty tired again tonite. I have to make a trip to the other end of the Island again tomorrow and then Wed. we will evacuate all of our patients. After that I suppose we will be busy taking down tents and turning in equipment. It will probably take us three or four weeks to get it all done. Tomorrow nite will be the last time we will open the P-X so I'll be out of a job after that. I'll have 27 dollars coming from this month and when I get paid I'll send it to you to get yourself a new dress or something else that you need to wear.

Honey I just heard the news and they said all 60 point men will be home by Jan. 1, so I should be coming home soon after that, don't you think. What do they say over the news back home about how soon the boys will be getting out with 50 points? We don't hear much over here. Gee I sure hope they do something pretty soon so I'll be eligible to come home.

Lieutenant Musick later received a letter from his wife that said Colonel Damron was discharged from the Walter Reed Hospital. He was home and was going to be an ear, nose, and throat doctor on March 1st in Elizabethtown, Tennessee. Merle was happy for the Colonel but cussing the War Department because he was still on Okinawa, and Colonel Damron was home.

October was quite a traumatic month for Merle and me, and our families didn't take it lightly either. While in California, I did not want to add insult to injury by spending the money Merle had saved for me, so I hustled on my own. Pay was good at the telephone company, and I was even able to save up, hoping my saving and thriftiness would provide some form of consolation for Merle. However, it didn't do much to console me. More and more I was missing my husband who I knew loved me with heart, body, and soul and told me in every letter he wrote. Even though he was upset about my moving with Valeria, I loved him very much because he was so kind and considerate of me. We had been separated far too long for just a couple of kids.

Good-nite, Darling! Sweet dreams and may God bless you Honey and keep you safe and sweet for me only! I say my prayers every nite for you and that we will be back together again very soon.

NOVEMBER 1945

Thurs Nite
Nov 1
My Darling!

No letter from you today Honey so my morale isn't so good tonite. The days are so long when I don't hear from you.

I did receive a letter from my folks today. Mother didn't have much to say except that Dad was taking his vacation that week. She said they received a nice letter from you and that she was going to write you that same day. I told them not to send anything for Xmas and now they think I'll be home by then but I'm afraid I won't make it. You know Honey I didn't even think about yesterday being Halloween until today when we were talking about it. Holidays don't mean anything to us over here because we don't have any way to celebrate. All we can do is think about what a good time the people back home are having.

Mother enclosed a clipping out of the paper about Howard Wilcox getting married. He surely didn't lose any time, did he? Well, he has been away 30 months so it is time he got home. He told me that they were going to get married soon as he got back.

Today all men with 60 points became eligible to go home. I wonder when we 50 point fellows will be eligible. I think about January. Boy they better get me home pretty soon or I'll go crazy.

Well Honey in a few more days I'll be a year older. I feel like 57 instead of 27. I need you to give me some young ideas mommy. I'll feel like I was 18 again when I get you back in my arms.

November 1st was officially the last day of the 74th Field Hospital. Many of the personnel unit and the medical unit left shortly thereafter with those of the Points Demobilization system. Merle also wrote that he was not part of the Field Hospital anymore. They were getting rid of the patients, and the next day, they would start packing the equipment. He expected that it would take about a month.

As soon as he got home, Howard Wilcox had married the same girl he had dated since high school. Presently, they live in Davenport after he spent most of his working life owning a grocery store in Waterloo.

On November 2, 1945, a plane crashed at the airport on Okinawa. Six men were on board along with the pilot. Merle was the first one on the scene.

I was going to clean up and shave after dinner but there was a plane crash at the airport. A C-47 made a crash landing and it was really a mess. There were six fellows in it plus the pilot. They were all hurt pretty bad but no one was killed. I was one of the first ones there and put all of them in my ambulance and took them to the 87th Field Hospital. It is 18 miles to there and it only took me 25 minutes so I really made good time over these rough roads.

The victims all survived.

At this point, Johnson and Gusler were still at Island Headquarters personnel center, waiting for their ship to come in. They were doing menial KP and helped maintain the center.

The next day, there was another bad accident, and Merle was called into action.

Honey I'm a little late in getting starting to write to you tonite because there was another bad accident. A jeep went over a cliff into the water with three fellows in it. We really had a job getting them out. We had to use a rope. Then I took them down to the 87th Field Hospital. I think they will all live. There has been five accidents here this week and most of them could have been avoided.

Merle wanted to go home so badly. He had most of the equipment packed but found out it had to be inspected first before it was turned in which meant more waiting. With all that waiting and nothing else to do, Merle had plenty of time to think, and it wasn't surprising when his thoughts would develop into worries and his worries into fears. He was always concerned about the number of marriage vows that had been broken between husbands and wives during the war.

What are you doing tonite Mommy? Are you writing me a real long letter? I hope so because your sweet letters are all that keep me going from day to day. I love you so darn much and am so lonesome for you. Honey, it makes me feel so good when you tell me how much you love me and how true you will always be to me. Darling a perfect home means everything and that is the only kind of a home I'll have. The only way to have a home is for both of us to be true to each other in every way. I've seen so much dirty work between husbands and wives since I have been in the Army that it makes me sick to think about it. Some people are worse than animals. I'm sure you can't blame me for being strict with you, do you Mommy? I just want to have a perfect home. I don't care for money or anything else but I want a happy and true home. How about you Honey?

At this time, I was in Oakland, California with Valeria, Mary Jane, and Ardys. I went to Harry James who put on a show at San Francisco's "Cow Palace." The four of us girls were thrilled with the show. Of course, I told Merle about it. He thought that was alright in spite of the fact that he did not want me in California in the first place. I knew I would never get him to see my side completely.

MERLE AND VALENTINA MARTIN

Thurs nite
Nov 8
My Darling!
Well Honey my morale is pretty low tonite. All my old buddies are leaving tomorrow. Weaver and I were down to Hdqtrs. today and I picked up the orders for Gusler and Johnson. They are leaving tomorrow and I'm going to take them down to personell center. I suppose they will be there a week or so before they get on a boat to come home. They are busy packing tonite and I've been helping them. I suppose we won't get much sleep tonite. Well I guess the sooner they leave the sooner I'll be eligible to go home. They are two happy boys.

I heard over the news tonite that men with 50 or more points that are in the States are eligible to be discharged. How about that? Isn't that dirty, and fellows overseas with 50 points aren't eligible to come home. Boy this army is really chicken shit. Surely they will do something for fellows like me pretty soon. I've got almost three and one half years in and 50 points too. I'll have 56 in Dec. I think I'll surely be eligible between Nov and Jan 1, and I'll still be home by the last of Jan. Honey, fellows like me have really gotten a dirty deal in this point system.

Johnson and Gusler, both with enough points, left for the personnel center the next day.

Well Honey this has been another busy day for me. I took Gusler and Johnson down to be processed and just got back an hour ago. It surely is lonesome around here without Johnson. We were really good pals. I am going to take their mail to them Sunday and spend the day down there. They will probably get on a boat sometime next week.

It was a bittersweet drive for Merle. He was happy to be transporting his friends one step closer to home, but he was not happy that he would be driving back alone. Merle visited Gusler and Johnson at the personnel center and continued to do so

140

every few days. They were getting upset too for being there so long and not having a boat to take them home. Merle was getting pretty irritated with Congress by this point and asked me to write our congressman so that he and the rest of the deserving soldiers could be brought home. Howard Cronkleton was Merle's new roommate, taking Johnson's place. Their food was still C rations which they couldn't stand more than they had to, so the two of them went to supply and made egg sandwiches and coffee after visiting Johnson and Gusler and had dinner at the personnel center. Gusler gave Merle his Australian-made alarm clock that day which was a welcome gift since Merle was getting up earlier.

Howard Cronkleton and Merle went to Naha for supplies for the boys including cigarettes. Merle wrote that they had bought some supplies and sold them for a little profit since they did not have a PX anymore. Howard and Merle split the $20 profit. He needed an outlet to do something since there were no poker games. No pay day meant no gambling.

Later on, they went to see Gusler and Johnson again. Their boat still had not come in. The boys were doing KP and cussing the War Department as usual. They had no idea when they would get on a boat, but both of them wanted to be home by Christmas. Merle was getting discouraged about his own trip home as he watched Johnson and Gusler continue to wait for their ship to come in. He wrote, "At this rate, I won't get home until July!" Of course, that did not sit well with me. I wanted him home by Christmas too. For me the war was over, and everything was finished except sending my husband home.

Wed Nite
Nov 14
My Darling!

No letter again today! My morale is pretty low tonite. Honey when I don't hear from you every day it makes me feel bad. I'd better get some mail tomorrow or else I'll start swimming home.

I worked a little today for a change. I greased my ambulance this morning and this afternoon took it down to the beach and washed it. Honey I really had to laugh. There were about twenty little native kids down there and they all wanted to help me so I gave them all some rags and let them do the work. You should have seen them--they were all over it and fighting to see who would do the most because they knew I would give them some cigarettes. They really gave it a good washing and when they finished I gave each of them a package of Camels. They will work all day for a bar of soap and a package of cigarettes. I guess I took cold down there in the water today because I am about froze tonite. It is real cold out tonite and the wind is blowing a gale so I'm going to get under the covers pretty soon. I have to go down to the other end of the Island again tomorrow.

Merle and Howard's ODs—wool winter uniforms—were issued with their Eisenhower Jackets on November 15th, just in time to get their ribbons sewed on before they left, not knowing at that point when exactly that would be.

Tues Nite
Nov 20
My Darling,
Well Honey I am a year older today. I thought I'd celebrate it by sleeping all day but they made me do a little work for a change. I was on duty at the airport all day. We have to keep an ambulance there every day so in case of a plane wreck. I guess I'll sleep tomorrow though because I don't have any trips to make as far as I know.
Honey I didn't get any mail from you today. I'm so down-hearted and no mail to cheer me up. I know it isn't your fault because you have some on the way to me. Maybe I'll get two or three tomorrow. Gee Mommy I'm so lonely for you. I wonder how much longer Uncle Sam is going to keep us apart. It hadn't better be long. It seems to me as if they aren't trying very hard to get the boys home from Okinawa. Most of the boys are still on the Island. I think Gusler and Johnson will both make it home for Xmas though. I get so down-hearted when I

even think about not getting home for Xmas. Just think Honey our wedding anniversary will be next month too and we will be apart again. This is really a cruel world.

When I get home we will have a lot of celebrating to do that we have missed out on--my birthday, our wedding anniversary, Xmas and New Years. I guess all we can do is not even think about it and look forward to the day we meet again. I can't help but think about it though--in fact that is all I think about. We have been apart so darn long. Honey we will really take life easy and do nothing but make love until we get caught up, and we will never catch up, will we Honey? Gee, Darling, I love you so terribly much and want to be with you so bad. Surely they will let me come home to you pretty soon. It is sure funny that married men aren't getting any consideration at all unless they have children. I can see that I've put in a year that I will never get any credit for unless they change things a lot.

I can't figure out why my letters were marked APO 226 because my A.P.O is still 902 and will be until I get into a different outfit. Honey in your newest letter which was Nov 9, you were going home after Sunday so I'm going to address this to Traer because you will be there by the time this letter does, and then you will have mail sooner. I hope that when you get back home you will spend all your time writing me love letters. You don't need to work Honey--you will be just as well off by staying home. Your allotments will be plenty to take care of you until I get there and then we can live on love.

Before his actual birthday, Merle received a Happy Birthday cablegram from me. It took six days to get it to him. I wanted to make sure he got it on time. Of course he was pleased because mail was coming so slow after the war was over. He was confused as to why he had a 226 American Post Office number for a while since he believed he was APO 902. I know now that he must have been considered for the occupation of Japan before the war ended.

Toward the middle of the month, General MacArthur announced that from then on, no one could send any money, and it had to be cleared by the commanding officer of the unit. Merle believed it was on account of the black market that was going on in Okinawa.

On November 15th, Johnson was finally on his way home. He would be followed by Gusler, shortly thereafter who was headed for Stuart, Virginia as soon as he touched American soil.

Thurs nite
Nov 22

    Well Honey guess this was supposed to be Thanksgiving, but it didn't seem like it to me because we aren't together. We had our turkey dinner today and it tasted pretty good only we didn't get much turkey. We did have a pretty good dinner considering that we are over here on Okinawa though.

Merle's Thanksgiving dinner that year was complete with turkey, cranberry sauce, potatoes, cherry pie, and chocolate cake. His belly got full, but it had shrunk since he had been overseas, so he could not eat as much anymore.

    Today was a quiet day. Everyone spent the day sleeping and it seemed like Sunday to me. The post office wasn't even open so we didn't get any mail. It has been three days now since I heard from you Honey and I'm really lonesome. I've been so down-hearted all day and I thought about how happy we were a year ago today. I thought about all the good times we have had together and I got so lonely that I went to bed crying. Darling I may be a big baby but I surely love my sweet Momma. I want to be with you so darn bad and they won't let me come home. Today over the radio they were telling about when troops in the States were considered surplus they were discharged regardless of points. I don't think that is a bit fair, do you? The Navy is lowering their points to 37 Dec 15 so that means more ships will go out of service. I guess they are forgetting all about us over here. The army is so slow. If they don't make me eligible to come home pretty soon I'll go crazy and believe me I don't have far to go.

Dear Valentina

Merle's mother wrote him and told him that Rath Packing Company was talking about going on strike for higher wages. News of strikes back at home seemed to dominate the radio, and Merle became more discouraged as conversations about bringing home the troops overseas began to decrease.

I just heard the news but they didn't say a damn thing about getting the boys home. All they talk about is strikes and things that will benefit the civilians. I guess they have forgotten all about us poor devils that won the war for them. They said today that effective today all meats wouldn't be rationed anymore. The only thing that is rationed now is sugar and automobile tires. I bet the people will really eat steak now for awhile. I wished all those damn politicians had to eat "C" rations for awhile like we do then maybe they would realize what we have been getting along on.

When Lieutenant Musick left, he gave his radio to Howard Cronkleton so that he and Merle could listen to the "Hit Parade" on Saturday nights. The show which was a favorite of many of us in those days played the old romantic songs Merle and I liked so well. He enjoyed the music, but it made him more lonesome for me. It seemed that listening to the radio was as entertaining as it was abusive for Merle.

Merle and Howard drew their winter OD (Olive Drab) uniforms toward the end of November. It was raining again that day, so they took two ambulances so their new outfits would not get wet. Merle's ambulance stopped running twice, and he had to get out and fix it. The Eisenhower jacket of his was pretty nice. It was certainly better than his other uniform that didn't fit. They picked their own jackets now, so they fit perfectly for the finest soldiers in the world.

Sun nite
Nov 25
I spent most of the day sleeping today--I was so tired and still am. This afternoon Howard C. and I went to Mass down at

the 87th Field Hospital. A Catholic priest came there to hold Mass at four o'clock. We were so surprised – a native woman and her little boy came to Mass and sit down in front. The mother seemed to understand perfectly and they stayed all through the services. They must have been in Hawaii sometime. She couldn't speak English but understood the sermon.

Tonite I went to the show – the first one in ages. It was pretty good too – Forget the Past with Fred McMurray. I suppose it was shown in the States in 1940 but it was new to me. I get so lonely sitting around that I'll go crazy if I don't get home pretty soon. The picture tonite was a love scene and it didn't help my morale a bit.

During his last few months on Okinawa, I requested one last favor of Merle. He knew I wanted white wool Navy blanket that had been used by patients when he got on the ship and promised that he would try to bring one home if it was possible.

I have one on my bed now but I don't know how to get it home. I can't send it through the mail because they examine all packages. I'll try to bring it with me but they will probably take it away from me. They are really nice. I used to get hold of quite a few when I was evacuating patients to the ship. There are quite a few things I'd like to have if only I could get them home.

But of course, above all else, I just wanted my husband back.

Fri nite
Nov 30
My Darling,
Well Honey another month has gone by – only 25 more days until Xmas. Gee what I wouldn't give to be able to spend the holidays with you. We were apart last Xmas and now we will be apart this one. We will be together in my heart though and you will be at my side every minute. Next year we will be in our little home and really enjoying life by this time next year,

won't we Honey? I'm getting lonelier and more down-hearted every day so they had better get me on my way home pretty soon.

DECEMBER 1945

Early in December, Merle received a letter from his mother who wrote him and told him the Rath Packing Company strike was settled with a 17 ½% raise for everyone. He also wrote me that he bought a brand new Japanese rifle. It was still packed in cosmoline to protect it, and it was worth a lot of money. According to Merle, it could kill at a distance of one mile, so it could be a deer rifle. It had wind gauge and a bayonet on it. I still have it today hung up high as a conversation piece since Merle was so proud of it.

Today has been a rainy day so I spent a good part of it sleeping. This afternoon I went to finish my deal on the Jap rifle and I got it too. It is brand new and hasn't ever been shot. Now I'm going to make a box for it so I can mail it home. I think before long that we will be able to get ammunition for them in the States and then it will be worth a lot of money as a deer rifle. I only have five dollars invested in it so don't care about selling it unless I get a big price for it.

We are still waiting for them to inspect our equipment so we can turn it in. I guess I'll be here until I come home. There is a rumor going around that the points will be lowered to 50 around Dec. 20 but we haven't heard anything for sure. Gee I sure wish they would do something to make me eligible pretty soon. It will soon be a year that we have been apart and that is long enough, isn't it mommy? I miss you so much Honey!

Honey I'm enclosing a money order for $20 for you as a little anniversary present. I want you to buy yourself something that you need with it. I'd send more but they check up on what we send home, and I want to send you an Xmas present. I'm sending it in plenty of time so you can go shopping before Dec.

15. Next year I'll be there so I can go shopping for you. We can have a double celebration then to make up for this one. I want to wish you a <u>very</u> happy anniversary Darling and in my heart we will be together. I'm going to write you a special letter about twenty pages long that day so you can be expecting it. You are such a sweet mommy and I am so proud of you.

It has been real cold out all day and we don't have any stoves so it isn't comfortable anywhere except in bed. Guess that is where I'll spend most of my time because I can keep warm in my bed. My cold is getting better slow but sure. I need a bath but am afraid if I take one I'll take more cold again. Maybe it will warm up again in a couple of days.

I suppose you are home and all rested up from your trip by now. Honey you will need all that rest when I get back so take it easy now.

Valeria decided to stay in California with Mary Jane, our other partner in our apartment in Oakland. The four of us had worked for the Bell Telephone Company. Ardys and I left together at the same time.

On December 7, Merle, Howard Cronkleton, and Russell Weaver played double solitaire. The guys had a lot of laughs like they were playing for a lot of money, according to Merle's letter. December 7th was also the fourth anniversary of the beginning of WWII with Japan. That was and is a sad day for me because I still remember it clearly.

Howard, Weaver, and Merle took pictures the next day. Then at four o'clock in the afternoon, they went to the Catholic mass at the 87th Field Hospital.

In the meantime, Howard's mother had taken it upon herself to get Howard out of the Army. She wrote to her congressman to let Howard be released since the war was over. Their commanding officer called Howard in and showed him the letter. Of course, he could not be let out. He only had 37 points. Howard was surprised when the commanding officer called him in and became slightly embarrassed as a result.

MERLE AND VALENTINA MARTIN

Thurs Nite
Dec 13
My Darling Momma!

Honey I received my first mail from you in thirteen days today. I was so blue and worried that I couldn't eat anymore. I hadn't heard from you since before you started home and I was so worried for fear that something had happened. I feel relieved tonite after getting two really sweet letters from you today. The letters I got today were written on Dec. 2, and 3rd. I am missing all those from Nov 23 to Dec 2. Anyway I know you arrived home safely and I'll get the other letters one of these days telling me all about your trip. I bet all the folks were glad to see you again and to have you back. I know I feel a lot better. Honey don't worry about getting a job. If you do be sure it is in a nice place, and I'd just as soon you wouldn't get one. Above all don't work at the Sinclair Station or any place like that. I know you don't need money so terrible bad. You will have plenty money after the Xmas shopping is over. Honey by the sound of your letters you did your shopping in a hurry. You are really on the ball, aren't you? I am really proud to know that I have a sweet mommy that takes care of everything and gets it done on time. Darling be sure you spend that $50 that I sent you on yourself for Xmas and get what you need to wear with it.

Santa Claus brought me another package from my sweet momma today. That makes two packages I have received from you and just what I needed too. Now I have plenty of toilet articles to do me until I get home. I'm going to save those T shirts and handkerchiefs until I get to the States. They are too nice to wear over here. If I tried to wash them I probably couldn't get them white again. Honey I'm going to smoke the cigarettes on our anniversary day and Xmas day and I'll think of my sweet Momma every time I puff on one. You were right about me needing a new billfold. My old one is going to pieces and the other day when I was washing my ambulance I dropped it into the water. Now it is cracking all over. It surely has been a good billfold and I wished I had all the money right *now that has gone through it. Remember lots of times I had over a thousand dollars in it.*

On December 14th, Merle received an anniversary card from me a day before our infamous December 15th anniversary the year before.

I later wrote Merle about a hometown serviceman we both knew, Earl Griffith, who was discharged after only twenty-eight months as a serviceman and no overseas duty. Merle was feeling badly because he had to stay on Okinawa while everyone else was going home.

Howard Cronkleton became a sergeant on our anniversary date. He was pleased because he had to look forward for several months of service. Merle felt bad because Howard had only 37 points.

On the 21st of December, Merle became eligible to go home. He started loading the equipment on a truck right away. There was one truck left at 6:00 in the morning, so he could get in two loads a day. He was ready to go now.

Fri Nite
Dec 21
My Darling!
Well Honey the good news finally came--I'll be eligible to come home Jan 1. I expect to be on the boat by the last of Jan. and maybe before. We can't leave until our equipment is turned in and that will be about Jan. 15. It won't be long anymore and it sure makes me feel good to know that I am eligible. We start turning in our equipment tomorrow. I have my truck all loaded and am going to leave early in the morning. I'll be busy every day now for a few days. Today I was so busy that I didn't even get my nap and I am really tired tonite.

I warmed some water after supper so I could shave and clean up a little. It warmed up a lot today and we were going around without a coat on. I hear over the radio that they have snow in Tokyo so guess the boys there will have a white Xmas too. One wouldn't know it was Xmas here because there are no decorations or anything. Guess it is better not to have any because we would only feel worse if there were things to remind us of it. Honey I wished you wouldn't have gone to all the trouble to send me another package because I probably won't get it before I leave. Anyway I have plenty of everything and I'll have to pack up quite a few things to send home because I won't have room for them in my duffle bag.

You brought me a sweet letter today and also a nice Xmas card. Thanks a lot Mommy dear. I'm so glad I know that you are thinking of me all the time. I also got a letter from my folks. They told me what they were getting you for Xmas. I'm sure you will like it and it will come in handy in our home.

So you are working steady now at Yordy's. How much does he pay you? It will be a little extra money and also help to pass the time until I get back.

Honey soon as I get back we will find a nice place to live-- that is the first thing we will do. I'm not going to get a job until we get all settled. Then we can take life easy and I can spend all my time making love to you.

Honey Mother said the new Buicks are out, why haven't you sent me a picture of them? I'd like to see what they look like.

You was wondering if it was a Mass or just a sermon that we were going to at four in the afternoon, well it is Mass. You see over here they have services whenever the Chaplain can get here regardless of what time it is. That is the only time he can get way down to this end of the Island. We are going down to Island Hdqtrs. to midnite Mass on Xmas Eve. They have built a new chapel and it is really nice. I'm going to take some pictures of it to send you.

I'm glad to hear that Ardys is going back to Cedar Falls. There is no use of her sponging from you. She is young and should be able to make her own living if she can't get along at home.

Honey why does Arlene B. come to you for help? If I were you I would let her worry about it herself. After all it is her own fault she got in bad. Maybe that will teach her a lesson. I wouldn't help anyone like that.

Dear Valentina

Well I suppose Johnson and Gusler are home by now with their wives – the lucky devils. I sure hope they get me started home pretty soon. I'm so lonely for you mommy. The time will pass pretty slow until I get on that boat.

Did you get a letter today? Honey I wished you would write me some long letters. The one I got today was only three pages long. Do you still love me as much as you used to? Mommy if you didn't I'd die because you are all I live for. I can hardly wait until the day we meet again. That will really be a celebration, won't it Mommy? It can't be much longer now. Just be an awfully sweet and true mommy to me so we can always have a happy home, promise Honey?

Well mommy I've told you all the news for tonite so I'll kiss you and get into bed because I have to get up early in the morning. I should write to the folks but I'll do that in the morning. Good-nite Darling! Here's a great big kiss for you to go to sleep on!

With all my love for you Honey, I'll always be your true and faithful daddy –
Forever & Ever
Merle
Honey please write me some long letters. I expect a 30-page on Xmas and New Year's Eve, please don't disappointment me.
God bless you Honey--may he bring me home to you in a hurry.

By the 23rd and 24th, men with 50 points were eligible, so Merle would have plenty of company on his journey home.

So you are reading "Forever Amber"! Honey that is a dirty book – you shouldn't read it. Ha! We had it over here. I read most of it.

So Arlene B. is three months along? She is really in bad shape. She should make the guy do something to help her. If nothing else he should divorce his other wife and marry her. It doesn't pay to mess around but they always get caught sooner or later. Isn't that right Honey?

I spent Christmas with Merle's brother, Edward, and his wife. Merle's parents were there too. To Merle, that day did not seem like Christmas. They had a turkey dinner and all the trimmings, but it just wasn't home.

Tues Nite
Dec 25
My Darling!
Merry Xmas Honey! I hope Santa treated you well. I suppose you had a big dinner today out at Edward's. We had a pretty good dinner too – turkey and all the trimmings. I am really full tonite. Howard and I just finished a sandwich. We got some white meat and saved it until tonite. It surely didn't seem like Xmas to me—guess it is because we are over here out of civilization and we can't be together. I saw only two trees decorated up on the Island. Howard and I went to midnite Mass last nite. I took my truck because about twenty fellows went. More than half of our boys are Catholics. We got back about three this morning so I slept until eleven.

After dinner today Weaver and I went down to the personell center to take down the names of all the fellows who have 50 points. I think we will be called by or before Jan 15 and if we are I should be on my way around the 20th. Gee mommy it really makes me feel good to know that I'll soon be on my way home to you. I get so excited thinking about it. It won't be long now Honey, until we will be back in each other's arms again and living a happy and peaceful life.

That day, men were alerted that there were 100 Japanese soldiers and three officers in the hills, all well-armed. Merle had his carbine with him and 500 shells. "Let them come!" he said. This was not an unusual situation. Every now and then, a few Japanese soldiers who had not yet given up would come out of hiding. The men opened their ammunition and became well-armed and ready. By morning, three or four thousand troops would round them up and patrol the hills.

DEAR VALENTINA

Two more trucks of equipment were now loaded to be turned in, so Merle was getting anxious to head for home. He wrote that he would draw his money when he was discharged. He didn't care about payday when they were processed. It would take about fifteen days to get to Seattle, they told him. He was ready and had been busy turning in equipment ever since he became eligible. Howard told Merle that he would send him any mail that came after he left. Howard himself expected to be home by Easter.

Well Honey they are starting to call in the 50 point men so I should be called by the last of next week. I surely hope so. I guess they expect quite a little shipping space by the first week in Jan. Boy I'll sure be glad to get on that boat and start for home. I guess it takes about 15 days to go to Seattle. I hope by the time I get there they have the place cleaned out and then I won't have to waste any time there. Honey we will really make hay when we get back into each other's arms. I think if I get discharged at Ft. Sheridan we will spend about a week in Chicago and then when we get home we can start looking for a place to live. What do you think about the idea mommy? Gee Honey I can hardly wait until I get you back in my arms again. You are such a sweet mommy and I love you so terribly much. How much do you love daddy tonite? Honey won't it be swell to have a home of our own and live a happy and peaceful life? I've almost forgotten what it seems like to be a civilian.

Honey today orders came in on our men with 52 points so I should be getting mine sometime next week. They expect to have most of the men with 50 points on the way home by Jan 10. Things are running pretty smooth down at the personell center and I guess they have plenty of shipping space for all eligible men. Gee Mommy it makes me feel so good to know that I will soon be on my way home to you. Honey by the time you receive this letter you can stop writing to me because after I leave our outfit I wouldn't get my mail anyway. I'll keep writing to you so you will know when I get on the boat or when I go down to the personnel center. Howard said he would forward all my mail to me after I left. He is sure a nice kid. I wished he had more points so he could go home with me. He should be on his way around Easter.

Sun Nite
Dec 30
My Darling!
　　Well Honey I've got some real good news for you tonite. This morning I went down to Hdqtrs. to see if there were any orders for us and there were. Weaver, Imbese and I all leave Jan. 3 to go to the personell center. I don't expect to be there more than four or five days before we get on the boat, because they have plenty of ships here now. We should be in Seattle before Jan 30. I was so happy and excited that I packed my duffel bag this afternoon so I would be all ready. I am sending some things home so my bag will be a little lighter. Now all I'm going to do until Thursday is lay around and take life easy so I'll be all rested up for the trip. I hope we get on a boat right away. It is so cold down at the personell center. All they have to stay in is some old tents and no stoves either. Honey I really didn't expect to get started home this soon. I'm so happy. It won't be long now until we will be back together again.

　　Boy I really cleaned house this afternoon. I had a real auction sale on my extra stuff. I sold my camera to Howard for a 100 yen (that is $6.66 in our money). I gave quite a few things away too. Tomorrow I'm going to get what Jap money I have changed into American money, guess I have about $40 worth of it.

　　Honey I received two sweet letters from you today, they were written Dec 18 & 19th.
So you got your Xmas present from Valeria. You said you hadn't opened it yet but the way you talk I bet you have peeked a little in order to have such a good idea what it is – you screwball! I know you better than that. Ha!

　　I'm glad you are getting along okay down at Yordy's. Don't work too hard Honey because I'll be coming home before long.

Dear Valentina

Mommy I have looked all over for another Parker pen but can't find any. There just aren't any more in any of the P-X's. If I do find one I'll get it though.

I must write to the folks tonite and tell them the good news too. I have owed them a letter for over a week but have been pretty busy every day. Now that my orders are in I'm all through working for the army. Someone else can do the work because I'm going to get rested up for that "Sentimental Journey". Ha! Gee Honey I can hardly wait, I'm so excited to know that I'll soon be making love to my sweet mommy again. That will really be a wonderful day when we meet again, won't it Mommy? How much do you love poppa tonite? I'm sure I know mommy but I just love to have you keep telling me. I love you so terribly much and am so proud of you. You always do everything so perfect. Honey someday we will have plenty of money but until then we will still live like kings and have every thing we need even if I have to work day and nite to get them for us. We both love nice things so we will never buy nothing but the best.

Well Honey I've told you all the news for tonite so will give you a great big kiss and write a few lines to my folks before I go to bed. I have to fix my bracelet too. I broke the hook on it loading boxes the other day. Mommy you have a good idea now when I'll be home so get prepared for the big event. I'll write you every day until I get on the boat. Be an awfully sweet mommy to poppa and look forward to the day when we are back in each other's arms again.

Good-nite Darling – I'll see you in my dreams. Here's a great big sweet kiss for you to sleep on.

With all my love for <u>you</u> <u>Honey</u>, I'll always be your true and faithful daddy –
Forever & Ever
Merle

January 1946

Tues Nite
Jan 1, 1946
My Darling!

   Happy New Year Mommy! I hope we can spend nearly every day of it together and I don't think we will miss out much either because I should be home by the last of the month. We missed out on a lot of fun last year but guess we should be thankful that we are both in good health. We will make up for what we missed out on.

   Well I suppose last nite was a big nite back in the States. I wished we could have been together and celebrated. Honey we will celebrate our New Year's when I get back, won't we? I heard over the radio that people were really acting crazy. Probably there were a lot of accidents. We spent a quiet evening playing rummy. I did stay up to see the old year out and the new one in. We had another turkey dinner today and plenty of it too. We probably will have stew all day tomorrow. This afternoon I packed my box of extra things to send home. Just think Mommy, one more day and I'll be started on my way home. I sure hope I don't have to spend much time at the personnel center before getting on a boat. I expect to be off the Island before Jan. 10.

   You brought me a really sweet letter today Mommy. I sure hope your cold is better by now. I have a cold myself. Those influenza shots we took didn't help a bit. I'm glad you got my package okay. Honey I'd send you a blanket if we had anymore around here. I found one but it had a big hole in it and is soiled pretty bad. We used to have quite a few around but they have all disappeared somewhere.

DEAR VALENTINA

Well guess there won't be any more 74ᵗʰ Field Hospital in another week. Most of our equipment is turned in now and the boys will all be transfered out pretty soon. After the 50 point men leave there will be about 60 of the men left.

Honey I'm glad you received the $50 money order, I wished you would have gotten yourself an Xmas present with it--that is what I sent it to you for. I'll buy you something nice when I get back.

So the Star-Clipper says I'm going to be discharged in January. They really know everything, don't they? I sure hate a small town because they always know everyone's business.

What are you doing tonite Honey? I hope you are missing poppa an awfully lot. I've been so lonesome for you all day, of course I'm lonesome for you every day though. Honey you can count on some first-class smooching from poppa on your birthday. We will really celebrate it in the good old-fashioned way, won't we? You are such a sweet mommy and I love you so darn much. I can hardly wait until I get you back in my arms again. How much do you love daddy tonite?

Well Honey I've told you all the news for tonite so guess I will give you a good smooching and go to bed. I have a cold myself and can't get warm. I'll write you again tomorrow nite.

Good-nite my sweet mommy! Here's a special New Year's Day kiss and also a wish that we will have <u>many many more</u> happy ones <u>together</u>. It can't be long now until we will be all settled and really enjoying life in a home of our own.

With all my love for You Darling, I'll always be your true and faithful daddy –
Forever & Ever
Daddy
Here's an extra big kiss for you, Honey!
Sweet dreams mommy! Always be awfully sweet to daddy!

Merle and Valentina Martin

Wed Nite
Jan 2
My Darling!

Well Honey tonite is my last nite in the 74th field. We are going to get up real early in the morning because we have to be down at the personell center by 7:00 and it is 60 miles. Guess we will leave about 5:00. Gee I sure hope it won't be long before I get on a boat. I want to be a civilian by Jan. 30. We probably will have an idea of how long we will have to wait by tomorrow nite.

Honey I got hold of a white Navy blanket today from one of the boys. I paid $3.00 for it. I packed it in a box and mailed it this afternoon so let's hope it gets home. If they find it I guess all they do is take it so we will only be out $3 plus the postage. It is a real nice one so I hope it gets home okay. I sent another package with some things that I didn't want to throw away.

I didn't get any mail from you today so there isn't much news. It is midnite now. All the boys have been stopping in to say good-bye to me all evening and I had to finish packing so I am pretty sleepy. You should see my duffel bag, it is really full. I have quite a few extra under clothes so when some get dirty I can just throw them away and I won't have to wash them out. The boys said that if any mail came in for us before we left they would send it to us, so maybe I'll hear from you again before getting on the boat.

I hope you are loving daddy an awfully lot tonite. Mommy it won't be long now until we can smooch each other in the good old-fashioned way and baby when that day comes we will really make hay, won't we? You are such a sweet mommy. I hope I get on a fast boat, if I do it won't take over fourteen days to go to Seattle.

Well Honey I haven't written much tonite but I'm going to kiss you good-nite and get some rest because we are getting up at 3:00 AM. I'll write you again tomorrow nite.

Good-nite Darling! Here's a great big kiss for you to go to sleep on. With all my love for you Honey, I'll always be your true and faithful daddy –

Dear Valentina

Forever & Ever
Merle.
Remember daddy loves you with all his heart – Always be awfully sweet to him.

God bless you Honey!
I'll be seeing you <u>soon</u>.

Fri nite 6:00
Jan 4
My Darling!
> *Well Honey here I am down at the personell center waiting for them to put me on the boat. I didn't write last nite because it was late by the time we got processed and a place to stay and there were no lights in the tent so I couldn't write last nite.*

> *When we were processed they said it takes 13 to 17 days to make the voyage. I was really surprised at the separation center they are sending me to. It is Fort Leavenworth, Kansas. I guess the reason is that they try to divide us up so about the same number go to each place. I can have you meet me at Omaha then and we can spend a few days there together before going on home. There is another boy from Austin, Minn., and he is going to the same separation center. I don't really care because they pay me five cents per mile to get home.*

> *This morning we were assigned to a unit and we are going to in the morning. I suppose it will be three or four days then before we get on the boat. You see they have to get our records all up to date. I'm sure we will be on the boat by next Wed. They may tell us tomorrow when we get to our unit when they expect to load on the boat. Imbese and I are still together and will be together until we get to Seattle. Weaver was put into a different unit. They aren't keeping the boys here any longer than it takes to get their records up to date because there are plenty of ships here.*

MERLE AND VALENTINA MARTIN

Honey I'm going to try to sell my watch on the boat because I think I can get $50 for it and I won't need it after I get home. That $50 will almost buy us a washing machine.

It is really cold down here in these old tents and we nearly freeze at nite. I sure hope we get out of here pretty soon. This afternoon Imbese and I went up to the 9th Station Hospital to take a warm shower and shave. They really have a nice hospital all set up in quonset huts just like stateside. It is going to be the only hospital on the Island after March 1, and the rest are all breaking up. We stayed up there for supper because they were having fesh roast beef.

Well Mommy are you lonesome for daddy tonite? In a couple of days you should receive my letter telling you that I'll soon be on my way home and not to write any more. I really miss your sweet letters Honey but I know it won't be long now until we will be together again so guess I can stand it. If we get any mail the boys will bring it to us while we are here so maybe I'll get a couple of letters from you before I leave.

Sat Nite
Jan 5, 1946
My Darling!

Well Honey this will be my last letter because I have some good news for you. Tomorrow morning we get on the boat and the boat is pulling out tomorrow afternoon. The name of the boat is "The U.S.S. Sea Marlin." It carries 2100 troops so guess it is a good ship. They say it takes around fifteen days to make the trip so we should be in Seattle by January 22. I'll send you a telegram soon as I can after we get off the boat.

I think I've really gotten a break to get on my way as soon as this, don't you think so Honey? I expect to be a civilian yet this month. Boy my morale couldn't be better than it is tonite.

Today when we got to this unit that we are going home they put us together according to separation centers and I ran into a lot of boys from Iowa. One of them is from Waterloo and used to work at Raths. After we talked awhile we found out both

162

of us know some of the same fellows back home. We really had a good visit talking over old times. He is married now and lives on Western Ave. I guess I'll have some company all the way now because we will be discharged together.

Well Honey we have to stencil our barracks bags and get our things all ready to go so guess I'd better give you a big kiss and get my work done. By the time you receive this I should be getting close to the States.

I hope you are loving daddy with all your heart Darling because that is the way I love you. It won't be long now until we will be living a normal life again and making love in the good old-fashioned way. Honey the next time you hear from me I'll be in Seattle.

Good-nite Darling! Here's a great big kiss for you to go to sleep on. Sweet dreams Mommy! We won't have to dream much more, will we?

With all my love for you Honey, I'll always be your true and faithful daddy –
Forever & Ever
Merle
P.S. Tell the folks I'll be seeing all of them soon. I didn't have time to write to them.

Be awfully sweet to daddy Honey!

God bless you Mommy dear! I'll be with you soon and in the meantime I'll be loving you with all my heart.

EPILOGUE

Merle arrived back in the United States about fourteen days after he wrote his last letter home. He did call me from Seattle, though sixty-six years later, I can't recall the exact day. The soldier who came home with him to Fort Leavenworth, Kansas was Russell Hagerstrom. Merle told me to contact Russell's wife so the two of us could come together on the Chicago Great Western Train from Waterloo. Russell's wife's name was Helen. I met her, and we became friends right away, likely due to our shared joy at seeing our husbands come home safe and sound. Much to our agony, the train stopped at every town along the way, and not surprisingly, neither of us could sleep well. The train wore at us as we traveled all through the night.

When Helen and I finally arrived at Leavenworth, Kansas we found the hotel where Merle and Russell had made reservations for us, and we went to bed at 8:00 in the morning. It was late afternoon when we woke up. When I walked down to the hotel lobby, I was shocked to see Merle looking out the front window, trying to spot me in the street. He and Russell had been waiting for us to arrive since noon. We were all shocked, elated, and then emotional about seeing each other. I couldn't believe he was real. That evening, we went to dinner and had our first meal together since December 1944. I don't remember where we went to dine, nor did I really care. All that mattered was that we were together again.

Merle was discharged on January 23, 1946 at Fort Leavenworth. From there, we immediately took the train to St. Joseph Missouri where we had been married four years earlier for a short honeymoon. We spent a day there as the happiest couple in the world before returning home to Waterloo the next morning.

Merle and Val, shortly after being reunited.

Snapshot of downtown Waterloo, Iowa on V-J Day, signifying the end of the war.

MERLE AND VALENTINA MARTIN

Just as Merle promised we would, we found an apartment of our own, bought furniture, and a new car. Our life was getting back to normal. I found a job at Black's Department store, and Merle started selling automobiles. As life progressed, we had a son born November 22, 1948, just two days past Merle's 30th birthday. Each of his grandparents, and all of my sisters adored our gift from Heaven.

When our son was a little over four-years-old, I went into real estate sales. Homes were in high demand in 1953—a home for every veteran.

After the war, we kept in contact with Merle's buddies and visited Gusler and his wife in Roanoke in 1949 and Johnson and his wife in Oak City, North Carolina. When our son entered Georgetown Law School in 1971, we visited Garabedian in Providence, Rhode Island.

Gusler eventually owned his own plumbing company. He was killed in a plumbing cave-in accident in 1975. His daughter, Mary Ann, died of ovarian cancer in 1995.

Weaver owned his own mechanic shop and service station for many years. He died in Kentucky in 1974. He was 54-years-old.

Wally and Velma remained married and worked for the *Los Angeles Times*. Shortly after Wally returned home, they traveled to his home state of Pennsylvania and adopted a baby girl. Later, they retired and moved to Albuquerque, New Mexico. We saw them many times when we passed through on our way to our winter home in Scottsdale, Arizona. They both passed away in the 1990's, she from lung cancer and he from heart issues.

Howard Cronkleton and his sweetheart eventually had five children, but we never saw them after the war. He and his wife are both gone now.

Howard Wilcox lives in Davenport, Iowa with his wife, Dorothy, who he eagerly married while he was still in an Army hospital in Clinton, Iowa.

Colonel Damron opened his eye, ear, nose, and throat office in Elizabethtown, Tennessee. He too passed away while he was still young.

Dear Valentina

Russell and Helen Hagerstrom built their own house in Waterloo, Iowa and lived there for the rest of their lives.

The Battle of Okinawa was never discussed again except with other soldiers.

My younger sister, Betty, who had written Merle a letter on toilet paper passed away in 1950 from leukemia. She was 21-years-old. When she died, she left a 10-month-old baby boy named Michael. He is a grown man now and has his own wife and children.

Valeria remarried in 1948, the same year our son was born. She had two boys and two girls: Greg, Stuart, Maurita, and Colleen. Today, Valeria lives a few blocks away from me in Waterloo, Iowa.

True to his word, Merle sat me on his lap when he was 80-years-old, and we loved each other as much as ever. In 2005, he passed away just a few days after his 87th birthday. Throughout our entire sixty-three years of marriage, he remained the same loving husband he had always been. In the time he was away, Merle wrote me over 300 love letters, each as genuine as the last. I have kept every one of his letters and reread them so that I could re-experience our lives from our third anniversary to the day he was discharged. I have read them so many times and every time I finish the stack, I still find myself waiting for him to come home.